"This is a book that will transform your family for generations to come. Inspiring, wise, and deeply motivating, *Adventuring Together* is a manual for parents who are longing for a deep connection with their kids, along with practical ideas for where to start."

—MANDY ARIOTO, PRESIDENT AND CEO OF MOPS INTERNATIONAL

"If a warm relationship with your kids is high on your priority list, you're going to love this book. It'll light a fire in your belly to take adventures and make memories in ways your kids will never forget."

—SARAH MACKENZIE, AUTHOR OF *THE READ-ALOUD FAMILY* AND HOST OF THE *READ-ALOUD REVIVAL* PODCAST

"Oh my, I love this book as it mirrors the very lessons we've learned as a family over the last eighteen years of parenting six boys. I'm not a natural adventurer, but I wholly believe in Greta's message: adventuring is parenting with connection in mind. So to that end, let's all make a little more room for adventure in our lives."

—RUTH CHOU SIMONS, MOM TO SIX, FOUNDER OF GRACELACED.COM, AND BESTSELLING AUTHOR OF *GRACELACED, BEHOLDING AND BECOMING,* AND *FOUNDATIONS*

"Greta's enthusiasm for promoting family togetherness and lasting memories through shared adventures sparkles in this lovely book. Whether you hike through a museum with a baby in a backpack or try to keep up with your teens on the backpacking trail, you'll find loads of encouragement and practical support for all kinds of daring and delightful adventures."

—JULIE BOGART, AUTHOR OF *THE BRAVE LEARNER*

"Greta Eskridge is inspiring a whole new generation of families to live outside the box and start exploring together. This book is a manifesto, not only for reclaiming adventure, but also for the very heart of our families."

—AINSLEY ARMENT, FOUNDER OF WILD + FREE AND
AUTHOR OF *THE CALL OF THE WILD + FREE*

"Equal parts truth and dare, *Adventuring Together* is the cheerful road map toward a more connected family. With the gentle wisdom of a gutsy tour guide, Greta Eskridge reminds us that memories are rarely made from the confines of a couch."

—ERIN LOECHNER, FOUNDER OF OTHERGOOSE.COM

"Greta leads the way on the trail to connect with our kids. Her stories are hilarious and her voice is welcoming, but her meaning is deep and rich: time, love, and fresh air make all the difference in the world to children. And our children desperately need us. Whether you've backpacked on the Appalachian Trail, or you've only ever hiked to Trader Joe's, Greta's book will take you by the hand and teach you how to invest in your kids through adventure."

—REBECCA FAIRES, AUTHOR OF *THE BOOK OF COMFORTS*, HOMESCHOOL
MOM OF SIX, AND DEDICATED FAMILY ADVENTURER

"Greta tells stories about the adventures that we all want to have with our kids, and then she gives us the tools. If you're like me and find yourself to be more 'indoorsy' than 'outdoorsy' you are in good company—this book is for you. Through this beautiful and honest work, she is going to inspire families and change relationships."

—RAECHEL MYERS, FOUNDER OF SHE READS TRUTH
AND AUTHOR OF *SHE READS TRUTH*

"Greta Eskridge is the friend you need shouting 'You can do this!' from the other side of the obstacle course. In *Adventuring Together*, Greta's words build confidence and courage to risk comfort and pursue audacious parenting. As you cultivate adventurous environments to bring out the best in your kids, you'll become a better version of yourself. So get outside, mamas. Greta has pioneered the way. You can do this!"

—MEGAN FATE MARSHMAN, INTERNATIONAL SPEAKER, AUTHOR OF *MEANT FOR GOOD*, AND DIRECTOR OF WOMEN'S MINISTRIES AT HUME LAKE CHRISTIAN CAMPS

"Everyone needs to read *Adventuring Together*. Parents, of course, but grandparents, aunts, uncles, teachers, mentors, youth leaders, and parents of teenagers, especially. Because Greta is here in the trenches of our modern world, walking in humility, honesty, and vulnerability. She lords nothing over, nor pontificates. She knows the hard work, the tears, the failures, and the near misses. But she presses on, knowing how important this is for *all of us*. If you need a fresh, fun, and approachable dose of inspiration for the work you do as parents, look no further. *Adventuring Together* is powerfully simple, profound in its implications, and potentially life-changing for all who read with a heart to connect with their children."

—REA BERG, FOUNDER OF BEAUTIFUL FEET BOOKS

"Here is the thing about Greta, she is an intentional and wonderful mother as well as a natural born teacher. I am so grateful she has combined both her skills as mother and teacher and shared them with us in this book *Adventuring Together*. This is an important book for any parent who is looking to make deeper connection and sweet, lasting memories with their children."

—HEATHER AVIS, AUTHOR AND NARRATIVE SHIFTER

Adventuring

TOGETHER

Adventuring
TOGETHER

HOW TO CREATE CONNECTIONS AND MAKE LASTING MEMORIES WITH *Your Kids*

GRETA ESKRIDGE

NELSON
BOOKS

An Imprint of Thomas Nelson

Published in Nashville, Tennessee, by Nelson Books, an imprint of Thomas Nelson. Nelson Books and Thomas Nelson are registered trademarks of HarperCollins Christian Publishing, Inc.

Published in association with William K. Jensen Literary Agency, 119 Bampton Court, Eugene, Oregon, 97404.

Thomas Nelson titles may be purchased in bulk for educational, business, fund-raising, or sales promotional use. For information, please e-mail SpecialMarkets@ThomasNelson. com.

Scripture quotations are taken from the Holy Bible, New International Version®, NIV®. Copyright © 1973, 1978, 1984, 2011 by Biblica, Inc.® Used by permission of Zondervan. All rights reserved worldwide. www.Zondervan.com. The "NIV" and "New International Version" are trademarks registered in the United States Patent and Trademark Office by Biblica, Inc.®

Any Internet addresses, phone numbers, or company or product information printed in this book are offered as a resource and are not intended in any way to be or to imply an endorsement by Thomas Nelson, nor does Thomas Nelson vouch for the existence, content, or services of these sites, phone numbers, companies, or products beyond the life of this book.

Library of Congress Cataloging-in-Publication Data

Names: Eskridge, Greta, 1976- author.
Title: Adventuring together : how to create connections and make lasting
  memories with your kids / Greta Eskridge.
Description: Nashville, Tennessee : Nelson Books, 2020. | Summary: "A modern,
  practical, and inspiring guide to creating deep heart connections with kids by
  regularly creating new experiences and intentional adventures together"-- Provided by
  publisher.
Identifiers: LCCN 2019049793 | ISBN 9780785231363 (paperback) | ISBN
  9780785231370 (ebook)
Subjects: LCSH: Child rearing. | Parent and child. | Activity programs in education.
Classification: LCC HQ769 .E766 2020 | DDC 649/.1--dc23
LC record available at https://lccn.loc.gov/2019049793

Printed in the United States of America

20 21 22 23 24 LSC 10 9 8 7 6 5 4 3 2 1

*To my darlings—James, William, Lilly,
and Davy—thank you for being the best
adventuring partners I could ever ask for.*

*And to my beloved Aaron—thank you for
encouraging me to adventure with our kids.
You've given me an incredible gift.*

CONTENTS

INTRODUCTION

The Stuff Lasting
Connections Are Made Of

All we have to decide is what to do with the time that is given us.
—J. R. R. TOLKIEN

I was sixteen years old when my dad asked me to go to India with him. It was to be a five-week trip, just the two of us. My mom and younger brother wouldn't go with us. They preferred the comforts of home to the certain discomforts we'd face while traveling in India. But I was different. My heart sang at the prospect of world travel. I'd never even been on an airplane before, and the thought of flying halfway around the world for my first flight made me giddy. Seeing new places, trying new foods, and meeting all kinds of new people filled me with intense excitement. I was more than ready for the adventure. And to embark on it with my dad.

There was a lot to do to get ready before we left. While my friends were wakeboarding around the lake, I was getting shots for diseases like typhoid and starting my malaria medication. While they were singing worship songs and holding hands around beach bonfires, I was babysitting and gathering garage-sale donations to fundraise for my trip. Some of my friends couldn't understand why I would give up time with them, give up my precious sixteenth summer. They couldn't fathom that kind of sacrifice. Maybe they couldn't fathom that kind of parent-child relationship either. "You're missing youth group summer camp for what?" I was asked over and over again.

But I was incredibly excited to spend all that time with my dad. I was a teenager, yes, but that didn't mean I dreaded the thought of five weeks alone with him. We had a close connection, one that didn't just happen. My dad nurtured our relationship from the time I was a little girl. Even though he was a self-employed dad of four and always short on time, he invested whatever time he could in creating heart connections with his kids. Year after year, moment by moment, memory by memory, he built our relationship into something strong enough to make me say a fast yes when he suggested I travel across the world with him for the summer.

This wasn't a spur-of-the-moment decision. I knew I wanted to spend that time with him because he had always shown up for me in simple, ordinary ways that stand out in my mind with crystal clarity even now. The voices of my friends and even the voice of society telling me, "Kids don't want to spend that much time with their parents," meant nothing to me.

Parents, don't be afraid to draw near to your kids! They want to be with you. They long for your presence. How many times does a toddler say to her mommy or daddy, "Watch me!"? How many times does a preschooler proudly showcase his LEGO-brick creation, crayoned drawing, or newest gymnastic trick? They just want us to be with them; they want to be welcomed into our world and for us to be interested in what they're doing. Our tweens and teens might not be able to express it as easily as our toddlers, but the desire is the same: "Mom, Dad, be with me."

Society tells you otherwise. Society tells you that your children will only draw farther and farther from you and that's normal and necessary and needed. That's a lie!

The fact is your kids need you more and more as they grow older. They need your time. They need your attention. They need a relationship with you! But relationships don't just happen. You have to build them. You have to be intentional. You have to invest in them.

And so often we parents don't do that. Then, when our kids don't really want to be with us, we are hurt, angry, or surprised.

That's when we tend to have these kinds of responses:

- **We freak out**. We backpedal and implement mandatory time together—which they resist because we haven't built any foundation for this time together.

- **We back off.** When they resist, we don't push through the awkward stage. We forget that relationships take time and trust to build and, instead of keeping at it, we just let our time together gently fade away.
- **We give up.** We believe the lie that this is how parent-child relationships go, and we just let our kids choose their friends and their music and their phones and their rooms over spending time with us.

So what can we do differently?

- **We can invest in them.** We can invest our time, attention, and love into our children's lives.
- **We can choose them.** We can choose them over our phones, our busy schedules, our golf dates, or our Saturday morning 5Ks.
- **We can show up.** We can show up time and time again. Even when they're not excited or it's inconvenient or we're all busy or it's raining.
- **We can be thoughtful.** We can put thought into the activities we invite them into and make those activities meaningful to our children specifically.

And we can accomplish all of this by adventuring together with our kids!

Adventuring together simply means getting outside the confines of your regular routine. Whether that means you are literally stepping outside the walls of your house and onto the hiking trail, like my family loves to do, or getting lost together in an adventure story, the key is that you are doing something different together. Those simple moments create lasting memories and connection.

That was my dad's gift to me, taking the humblest of moments and turning them into a grand adventure. Any trip, event, or even a moment held the potential for becoming a meaningful connection. By being faithful in the little things, he made a big impact on my heart.

Adventuring together simply means getting outside the confines of your regular routine.

We live in a day and age where there are so many things vying for our children's attention and, even more, for their hearts. There is an endless array of activities to take part in, texts to send, and the newest shows to binge-watch on Netflix. There are new apps to explore, and there's the societal need to keep up with the fun that friends, acquaintances, and even strangers are having. All these things can create distance between our hearts and the hearts of our kids.

Whether you are a parent of preschoolers or high schoolers, this book offers you the first steps to lessening that distance and connecting with your kids in a deep and meaningful way. I'll help you find ways to create, maintain, and grow lasting connections, all through adventure!

Remember, you don't have to fall prey to growing apart from your children. That doesn't have to be your story! But in order for that not to happen, you must be intentional and put in the work. Building relationships takes time and presence, not splash and flash. It takes space outside your normal every day to make it happen. Adventuring with your kids creates that space. Adventures provide a dedicated time together to talk, grow, laugh, and learn. Best of all, adventures make memories, which is the stuff lasting heart connections are made of.

So let's make a plan! Let's get out on the trail, take a cooking class, or start a book club. Let's adventure together!

Part 1

HOW ADVENTURES
MAKE CONNECTIONS

Chapter 1

ADVENTURES CHANGE US

Inside all of us is Adventure.

—MAURICE SENDAK

We took up much of the room on the waiting platform, repeatedly warning our excited, curious kids to stay behind the yellow line and not get whooshed away by a speeding train. Our big group of mamas and kids stood out from the crowd of regular metro riders. People looked. Some people stared. Others smiled at us. The kids didn't notice. Or care. For most, it was their first time riding public transportation. They studied the map of the route, finding where we'd get on and asking where we'd get off. We were having an adventure, and they were so into it.

The train pulled up, and we mamas nervously checked, rechecked, and then checked again that it was the right one. Even as we stepped aboard the metro, there was a little lingering fear: *What if it's the wrong train?* Then the doors slid shut, and the new worry became, *Do we have all the kids?* Swallowing my nerves, I counted. One in a stroller and two more holding the handles. Mine were accounted for. The metro lurched forward, and we lurched with it.

The metro cars were warm and crowded inside. The mamas looked at each other with dismay. It was a long ride to downtown Los Angeles, and none of us wanted to split up. We had no choice, though. Holding our little people near and ignoring their requests to sit with their friends, we all walked awkwardly through the train, looking for at least a few seats together. When I found a spot to park the stroller, I unbuckled Lilly and instructed my boys to share a seat by the window.

James was content to sit and gaze at the view, but Lilly and William already wanted snacks. The sign on the wall said clearly No Eating or Drinking. I didn't know how seriously those rules were to be followed. This was my first time riding the LA metro, and I figured I didn't need to make more of a scene than I already was, so I tried to distract my hungry kids with toys and watching the world speed by out the window. I had a feeling it was going to be a long ride.

Our group had been adventuring together for a couple of years. What began as simply a way to engage our kids in outdoor learning once a week quickly became a way of life. We called ourselves the Adventure Club. We had grown used to strapping babies on our backs, stuffing backpacks with snacks and diapers, and hiking dusty trails together. We'd gotten more confident with each hike. We found ourselves impressing fellow hikers on the trails. They couldn't believe this troop of mamas, babies, toddlers, preschoolers, and first graders was hiking the same trails they were. We couldn't either! But it sure felt good. We eventually expanded our adventures to include tide pool visits, trips to the beach, and even some museum tours. We had never, however, braved anything like the metro.

Taking public transit to downtown LA, leaving our cars behind, carrying everything we needed in our strollers or purses, and traveling through some gritty urban areas, all with a passel of small children, felt somehow more nerve-wracking than hiking a trail with mountain-lion warnings ever had. It was new. New was good. But new was also a stretching experience. Being stretched isn't easy.

When our metro car entered a dark tunnel and we went underground, all the kids cheered. Most of our fellow passengers had their headphones on and took no notice. But some passengers smiled. They took pleasure in the delight of our kids. These were the makings of lasting memories. I knew our kids would not forget their first subway ride. It didn't matter that we weren't riding the famed subways of

New York City or the beautiful, tiled subways of Paris. They were perfectly happy where we were.

We raced along through the darkness, and the kids stared out the windows, mesmerized. All too soon the car came to the end of the line, and it was time to get out and change trains. We gathered our belongings and our kids and rushed to find the new metro line. After we found our platform, we all breathed a little easier. One more stop and we'd be done! We would have successfully navigated Los Angeles's public transportation with a bunch of kids in tow.

Our metro pulled up with a whoosh of cool air, the doors slid open, and the kids swarmed inside. They knew what to do now. The metro car was empty, except for a person in a wheelchair at the very end. We settled into our seats, the doors shut, and we were on our way. The lights from the tunnel began rushing by.

That's when we noticed it. A powerful odor coming from the body hunched in the wheelchair down at the end of the car. Before my kids could say anything out loud, I pulled them close and whispered, "Sometimes people can't take baths. I know it smells bad. Just pull your shirt over your nose if you have to and look out the window."

I looked around the car and saw many heads bent together. No doubt other mamas were having the same kind of conversation. This was a part of riding the metro that I hadn't anticipated. It wasn't easy. The man or woman in the wheelchair was completely covered with dirty blankets, save two thin, filthy legs clad in tattered socks and sandals.

There was no movement, and it was hard to think about the condition of the human being huddled under the blankets. The smell was awful. My kids were overwhelmed by it and wide-eyed at this new experience. I tried to help them, urging understanding and compassion while also trying to show compassion for their feelings and discomfort.

When the metro pulled into our stop, we exited, breathing in great gulps of stale underground air and wondering what would become of that person under the blankets. None of us knew exactly how to handle that situation. But at the very least, we knew it was going to be fodder for some good talks about things like compassion, understanding, and grace for people who are different than us. That adventure on the metro was going to help us grow.

THE GIFT OF DISCOMFORT

Adventures change us. They take us out of our routines, our homes, our neighborhoods, our people—and make us grow. Adventures are so much fun. And we want that! But it's when the adventures go beyond just being fun and push us into uncomfortable places that we are offering a great gift to our children. Because out of that discomfort comes all kinds of valuable learning about

> It's when the adventures go beyond just being fun and push us into uncomfortable places that we are offering a great gift to our children.

themselves and the world around them. Best of all, when we walk with our kids through the discomfort, it pushes us together, growing our relationships even stronger.

That ride on the metro reminded me of my first few days in India as a wide-eyed teen. There was beauty everywhere. Jasmine flowers hanging from the beautiful braids of little girls, bright-colored saris, and sassy monkeys jumping from rooftop to rooftop. But there was also poverty and need like nothing I had ever seen. I knew what it was to have need but had never known hunger or homelessness. In my world back home, shopping at the thrift store for "new" clothes, struggling to pay bills, or having only one car to drive meant we weren't well-off. In India, being poor meant living under a roof made of cardboard and torn pieces of plastic. It meant begging for food and sending your child to sift through piles of trash for bits of metal or glass that could be sold for a pittance.

Those first few days of walking to the market, past trash piled on the side of the road, I pulled my shirt to my nose and tried not to gag. I glimpsed mice and rats darting through the trash piles. And one time, I saw a baby sitting alone on one of those piles; her mother was nearby digging for anything worth selling. I was heartbroken and shaken to my very core. Within days of being there, my perspective on what it meant to be truly in need changed utterly. My perspective on almost everything that mattered changed utterly. It was one of the best things that ever happened to me.

That growth I experienced in India was often uncomfortable. Oh sure, many parts were fun, exciting, and absolutely wonderful. But there were parts that broke my heart. Much of the trip brought up lots of questions and conversation between my dad and me.

On a much smaller scale, my kids experienced this when we rode the metro to LA. They loved that moment when the subway went underground. But other parts, like walls covered with graffiti and views that were gritty and urban, brought lots of questions. Even more, the person on our train hunched over in a wheelchair, covered with blankets, and reeking of urine was cause for concern, sympathy, and learning to be bigger than our feelings. All of it brought growth for us as we walked through it together.

GETTING OFF AUTOPILOT

The thing that makes adventures such powerful change agents is that they get us outside our normal routine. When adventure shakes up our regular routines, every part of us feels the impact. Change engages all of our senses: we see new things, smell new aromas, taste new foods, hear new sounds, and feel new things physically and emotionally.

One of my favorite things about going on an adventure with my kids is that we're not walking through the day on autopilot. We're more fully engaged with the world around us and with one another. This is incredibly important to me, because we are living in a time where all of us are becoming less and less engaged with things like nature, books, and face-to-face relationships. I want my kids to smile and say hello to the strangers we pass on the hiking trail, instead of never seeing them because they're looking at a phone screen. I want them to look up and see a hawk soaring overhead or the way thunderheads are forming over the mountains. I want them to get lost in a story we're reading together instead of getting lost scrolling through pictures on Instagram. I want my kids to be changed by the world they live in and the people and ideas they encounter. But that will never happen if they don't go out and experience the world.

We can't simply blame the disconnection and lack of engagement we feel with our kids on technology and busy schedules. Instead we must be fully honest with ourselves and ask:

- Are we spending thoughtful, quality time with our kids? When we do, are we present, engaged, and welcoming?
- Are we willing to walk through discomfort with our kids in order to better connect with them?

If we can't answer yes to those things, then we have to make a change. We have to begin making investments of our time, energy, and attention into the lives of our children. And then we can begin to create the kind of connection both we and they are looking for.

THE HARD WORK OF RELATIONSHIP

Of course, getting out and experiencing the world is not always easy. It takes commitment to start and then commitment to stay the course when things get uncomfortable or even truly difficult.

When I began having regular weekly adventures with my kids, it was a lot of hard work. I had a five-year-old, a three-year-old, and a one-year-old. I had a nervous husband who worried about me adventuring all alone with our three young children. And, every time we went out, I had to haul a backpack full of water bottles, enough snacks to feed a small army, and plenty of diapers and wipes for trail potty stops. To complicate things, before too much longer, I was pregnant again. But I didn't want to give up our adventures. It was often sweaty and exhausting work, but I found that, time and time again, it was worth it. These adventures were changing us. My kids began to grow their own adventurous spirits, and, even more exciting to me, their hearts were becoming more and more connected to mine.

It's always been my prayer that my relationships with my kids will last past childhood. I want to reach the teen years and have the same kind of close bond with my kids that I had with my parents when I was a teen. I want to reach the college years and even the adult years with kids who still want to be with me. I want them to feel safe coming to me with the hard questions, with their fears, their discouragements, and with their dreams. However, I know that if I want to create these lasting relationships with my kids, I have to prove to them that they can trust me. And what I have seen is that this kind of trust is being built every time we adventure together.

When we get lost on a hiking trail, or on a freeway while driving into the city, they learn that together we can work through that hard thing. They see me stop to pray—and remind me not to close my eyes if I'm driving—and ask God for peace, safety, and help. Then I ask them for their help and ideas. If one of us is nervous or scared, we comfort each other and remind one another to stay calm. And when we figure our way out, we all celebrate together. We grow a little bit with each struggle.

When we adventure, my kids realize that the world is much bigger than the suburban neighborhood we live in or even the wilderness parks we visit.

We also grow more prepared to handle the next challenge that will inevitably come our way.

I truly love the fun and excitement of adventuring with my kids. But even more than the fun, I value our adventures, because through them we can grow together. When we adventure, my kids realize that the world is much bigger than the suburban neighborhood we live in or even the wilderness parks we visit. They learn that different and hard don't have to be scary. Instead, they see that different and hard can lead to beauty and strength.

If I can walk through all this alongside them, answering their questions and helping them if they feel uncomfortable or nervous, then I am parenting with connection in mind. Adventuring together gives us the opportunity to open up our hearts to one another and to the world around us.

Chapter 2

YES, YOU CAN ADVENTURE WITH YOUR KIDS!

I don't like to doze by the fire. I like adventures,
and I'm going to find some.
—LOUISA MAY ALCOTT

We have all seen those pictures of adventurous families climbing glaciers together, ice crampons on their feet, backpacks full of gear on their backs, and brightly colored helmets on their heads. We've watched videos of families with two toddlers, three preschoolers, and twin newborns embarking on yearlong RV trips from the northern tip of North America to the southern tip of South America. In response, maybe you've thought, *I'm just struggling to get through a grocery-store trip with my kids. That's all the adventure I can handle right now.*

Well, guess what, mama? This book is for you!

Because it's not the location or the altitude, the ruggedness or the heat, the number of kids you have trailing behind you or the number of days that it's been since you showered, whether you're sleeping in a tent or in that fancy RV that make the adventure count. It doesn't matter if you've never hiked or never dared to take your preschoolers to a museum. What matters is that you are with your children, that you are spending time together face-to-face or shoulder to shoulder. And that, during the time you are adventuring, you are making memories and building connections between their hearts and yours.

As I set out to write this book, I wondered more than once if I was qualified to write on adventure. After all, I've never climbed a mountain. I took my first backpacking trip at the age of forty-two. My kids haven't been to Iceland. They haven't even hiked the depths of the Grand Canyon. Two of them have never been on an airplane. I don't do open ocean swims or train for triathlons. I ran a half marathon once. It was the peak of my fitness accomplishments. I don't own ice crampons or snowshoes. I'm actually afraid to even drive in the snow. When I waded in a creek a few years ago and caught my first frog, I acted like I had wrestled a full-grown alligator. I've only visited a few of America's national parks. I despise vault toilets and loathe camping trips where I can't get a shower after a few days.

The truth is, my adventure credentials aren't that amazing.

But here's the thing I keep coming back to: I love adventure. I love it so much! And I love adventuring with my kids. I love connecting to their hearts through all the pretty tame adventures we have together. I know they're tame because there are no shortage of incredibly adventurous Instagram accounts to compare to my own. So it's easy for me to wonder, *Am I really qualified to write this book? Will anyone take me seriously? Aren't there a hundred other mamas who are far more adventurous than me who should be writing this book?*

Maybe.

And that's okay.

I'm writing this book for the rest of us mamas. For the one who's never taken her kids on a hike. And who wonders if she can. For the one who can't afford to take her kids on exotic adventures. The one who hates camping and can't fathom peeing in the woods. The one who doesn't like driving in traffic and is too nervous to take a road trip without her spouse. I'm writing for the mama who is terrified she'll see a snake on the trail. Or that she'll get lost on a city subway or a country road. The one who isn't in the best shape. And the one who doesn't even own a backpack.

I'm here to say, "Mama, I am just like you. My little adventures with my kids are still making big connections, and you can have that too!"

Remember, to adventure with your children you don't have to:

- Be a CrossFit mama.
- Be exceptionally brave.
- Have an extensive knowledge of flora and fauna.
- Love the ballet.
- Be a backpacker.
- Not be afraid of snakes.
- Be a nature lover.
- Travel the world.
- Love camping.
- Be a crunchy mama.
- Sleep under the stars.
- Be a mama who makes playthings out of sticks and moss.
- Have taken martial arts or cake-decorating classes.
- Be an outdoors woman.
- Know all about fine art.
- Be a hiker.

All you need is a willing heart and a desire to connect with your kids. The rest will follow.

JUST GET OUT THERE AND DO IT

It was going to be our longest, hardest hike yet for the Adventure Club. A waterfall hike with creek crossings, a distance of more than four miles, and a lot of elevation gain for the little legs that would be walking it. Some of us moms would be carrying newborns on our chests and nursing on the trail. Others would be hauling heavy toddlers on our backs. All of us would be carrying extra snacks and water, because we'd learned long ago that it was never good to run out of either.

> All you need is a willing heart and a desire to connect with your kids. The rest will follow.

The air was cool, and our legs were fresh as we started down the trail. We took in views of the pine tree–filled mountains stretching down to the suburban sprawl of the valley below. The creek, full from winter rains, rushed past us. The kids were laughing and running. The mamas were exclaiming joyfully over the green hills and beautiful, blooming California lilacs. We were off to a great start!

While we walked, other hikers passed us. They were often wearing hiking boots and carrying hiking poles. Many of them had cool gear, like backpacks with water bladders inside of them. (Imagine a big hot-water bottle with a straw attached to it, except filled with cool water and so much more easily accessible than the water bottles we'd have to dig out of our backpacks every time the kids were thirsty.) Meanwhile, our kids were hiking in Crocs clogs,

Converse sneakers, or whatever shoes we could find for them as we rushed out of the house that morning. None of us had a legit hiking backpack and certainly no hiking poles. Our group stuck out like a sore thumb amid those serious hikers.

We were quite the spectacle, five or six moms and what felt like fifty small children on a narrow dirt trail. Not one of us was a truly experienced hiker. We didn't have wilderness first aid training. Or a list of famous trails we'd conquered. What we did have was a passion to get our kids outside and to help them develop a love for nature and hiking. Even though our kids were still young, we wanted to use our time with them wisely, to make the most of it. And what we were quickly discovering was that connections of all kinds flourished when we adventured together.

Hiking was one of our favorite adventures. We loved to see our kids connect with the outdoors. As they became comfortable and familiar with nature, they began to love it. They learned the names of plants and trees and butterflies. They thrilled at the sight of a tarantula or a snake. They delighted in the excitement of new trails and the familiarity of old ones. Nature became a friend.

They also connected with one another. They formed and cemented friendships as they walked side by side along the trails. It was a common sight to see our kids, hand in hand, skipping, giggling, and just enjoying the magic of spending time together. Weekly adventures grew such strong bonds among all the kids in the group. The relationships were not forced but grew as organically as the wildflowers blooming along the trail.

And, of course, just as we hoped would happen, our kids connected with us too. Sometimes a little one would need our hand to hold while climbing the steep parts of the trail or over big rocks. Then the hand would stay in ours as we walked, talking about the birds we saw or wondering what was ahead. Or one of our older kids would wait for us to catch up, excited to show us a crop of wild cucumber or a lizard. Every week we made new memories together, and those memories knitted our hearts together in such lasting ways. It was never the magnitude of the adventure or the mileage of the hike that made the memories count. It was just the fact that we were out there together, making it happen over and over again.

When we got to the first creek crossing, we found the water was moving a lot faster than we were used to. In Southern California, our creeks are often a trickle. But it had been a wet winter, and the snow melting far up in the mountains made for full creeks. There were rocks for stepping across and keeping feet dry, but many were completely covered and others were wet and slippery. We didn't want any of our kids falling in that cold water. But it was going to be hard to get them across while also keeping ourselves dry. I was seven months pregnant, and my balance wasn't so great. My friend Jana was carrying her six-week-old daughter. Tricky.

As we stood there assessing the situation, unwilling to

turn back but not sure how to move forward, some of those other hikers on the trail came to our rescue. A few of them asked to take our kids' hands and then waded into the water to help them across the slick stones. Then they helped us mamas with babies on our backs, our fronts, or in our bellies. After I crossed, I looked back and watched the scene before me.

There were kids on one side of the creek and kids on the other, with people standing in the water helping everyone cross safely. The kids were cheering. Our new friends encouraged them to keep going when they were scared. It was really one of the most beautiful sights, those friendly hikers caring for and helping us all. Our adventure that day created connections even among strangers.

We all felt pretty awesome after making it past that obstacle. It would have been so easy to turn back. After all, we were just a bunch of mamas with a whole bunch of little kids. We'd already hiked a fair amount, and no one expected more from us. Except for our kids. And we expected it from ourselves. So we went on.

We came to another creek crossing. It was easier this time. We had a confidence boost from that first treacherous crossing. We climbed uphill, crossed the creek again, and then heard the roar of the waterfall ahead. We couldn't see it yet, but hearing it thrilled us. We pressed on, rounding a corner of the trail. Then there it was! Loud, flowing full, and sending out a cool mist as it thundered into the pool below. It was what we came to see.

The only problem was that between us and the falls lay the biggest creek crossing yet! Much bigger than that first one. And this time there was no one around to help us. The water was moving fast. There were lots of rocks to maneuver over or around. We stared at the falls longingly and decided. We weren't turning back.

I hiked up my maternity pants, grabbed my two-year-old by the hand, and waded in. My boys, four and six years old, moved ahead of us with another mama who had a free hand to offer to them if they needed it. We'd all be hiking back to the car with wet shoes, but it just didn't matter anymore. None of the kids seemed scared at this creek crossing. Their confidence had grown, and the falls were luring them forward. I slipped a few times but didn't topple in, and then we made it. It was the greatest feeling to walk up to the base of that waterfall, to hear the roar of the water and feel the mist on our faces. Every bit of the hard work and effort we exerted to get there was worth it.

> You just have to get out there and do it.

I'm so grateful for the past ten years of adventures just like that one. Our list of adventures, and all the stories that go with them, make it easy to answer when asked, "How do you hike and adventure with babies and toddlers? It just seems so hard."

My response is always the same: "You just do it."

The truth is, there is no magic formula or any special tricks to adventuring with your kids. You just have to get out there and do it.

You carry babies on your front and backpacks loaded with lunches and snacks on your back. And then, when the babies get too big for the front, you carry them on your back and the backpack goes in front. It's hard work. You get sweaty and dirty and sometimes cranky (or maybe that's just me). You don't look cute or fashionable (or maybe that's just me). You train the toddlers and preschoolers to carry a backpack with their own water and snacks. And sometimes you carry all the backpacks and the baby when the hike gets too long. You bring candy as a bribe for the desperate moments that sometimes come when it's so hot and you're all so tired and there is still a mile left of the hike.

You dole out the candy one piece at a time to keep them quiet when the ballet is too long. You teach them to not touch priceless pieces of art and what the line in front of all the paintings means in an art museum. You read them books that are above their reading level because you know the good story will draw them in. You take road trips without any other grown-ups and trust that they'll help you stay awake on the long stretches. You go camping without your husband and hope the kids will be able to help you get the tent up. You drive to the city, even though traffic and crowds make you nervous. You walk to the donut shop on Saturday mornings, because traditions build memories.

You start with short hikes and simple adventures, and then you just build on them. And before you know it, your kids will amaze you with their tenacity and enthusiasm to push through challenges and try new things with you.

DON'T GIVE UP!

I'll have the picture of us standing in front of those falls forever tattooed on my heart. Us proud mamas with arms around one another, wind blowing our hair, and the biggest, proudest grins on our faces. Our kids lined up in front of us in a wobbly line, so little and so fierce. We made it! Without hiking poles, waterproof boots, or even fully knowing what we were getting ourselves into, we made it. And even though we had only hiked a couple of miles, and now, looking back, those creek crossings seem utterly tame, at that moment, we felt like we'd climbed Mount Everest. A small adventure for others and a big one for us. It's all about perspective, isn't it?

Of course, after that triumphal moment in front of the falls, we still had over two miles to hike back to the car—with wet shoes, wet shorts, and tired kids. It wasn't going to be easy. We waded back through the rushing creek. We stopped to exclaim over a California newt and a bright blue dragonfly discovered near the water. We took more frequent water breaks, rested in shady spots along the trail, and dug in our backpacks for leftover snacks. The kids weren't the only ones who were tired. My legs ached from hauling my big baby belly along the trail. I was worn out.

Finally, we neared the end of the trail. Unfortunately, it was the worst part. This was one of those terrible hikes that ends with a long, steep, uphill climb. It was afternoon, and the sun was hot. There was no shade, no cool creek to cross, and no respite from the relentless incline. All the kids were complaining. Some refused to walk anymore. Mamas gave piggyback rides. We encouraged the kids who were far too big to carry to keep going by handing out jelly beans and M&M's one at a time.

My little Lilly, only two and a half years old, was utterly worn out. I couldn't carry her in a backpack because my pregnant body couldn't take the extra weight. So she had hiked the whole trail, and she had not complained once. But as we climbed that hill, she was done. Lilly sat down right in the middle of the trail. "Mommy, can't you carry me?" she begged. I looked at her with so much love and genuine sadness.

"Baby girl," I told her, "Mama can't carry you. I have this big baby in my belly, and there is no room for me to carry you too. You have to walk the rest of the way by yourself."

She looked at me and said sadly, "But Mommy, I'm just a little girl."

I wanted to scoop her into my arms right at that moment and run to the top of the hill. I didn't want her to have to do it anymore. The thing is, she had to. There was no way out but up. And with a lot of coaxing and a lot of time, my adventurous little warrior made it to the top. I didn't go into early labor, and she didn't give up. We had worked our way up to that moment. By showing up every week to hike with me and her small friends, little Lilly had been training for this day. No, we didn't summit a mountain, but we did take a step in that direction. Nine years later, when she is struggling with something hard, I remind her of this day. I tell her she was strong and brave and tenacious when she was two, and she still is today.

"You just did it, Lilly. You climbed that hill."

So, if you've been wondering if you can do it, if you can adventure with your kids, now you know. You can. You just pick up your backpack, strap on your kid or snap on your seat belt, don't forget the snacks, and go. Even when it is hard and scary and overwhelming and new and you are underprepared, you still try. You show up over and over again, and you make those adventures happen. Because you know the connections that come out of the adventures are worth it every time.

Part 2

START THE ADVENTURES

Chapter 3

Start Small

> Not all of us can do great things. But we can
> do small things with great love.
> —MOTHER TERESA

When my kids and I began adventuring, we didn't start with the big adventures. We started with well-marked trails at the nature center. At first, I felt disappointed in our seemingly small efforts, but starting small was actually the critical component to our growth. Setting our sights first on small, doable adventures built our confidence and ensured that we would keep on adventuring together, making memories and heart connections along the journey.

I still recall all the details of that first adventure, when we drove to a nature preserve not too far from home. It was late in the day, but the air was hot, heavy, and still. We stopped at the nature center to get a map and directions for a hike. The docent pointed out a trail that wasn't too long. "Be sure you are back before sunset," she told me. "There are mountain lions here, you know."

I just smiled, full of confidence and excitement. We were there for adventure! I wasn't afraid.

The trail led us away from the nature center, and soon all we could see were golden rolling hills dotted with oak trees. We were alone, and it was just what my heart had been longing for. There was a rustle in the dry grass next to the trail. We all jumped a little. A tiny bunny hopped away from us. The boys exclaimed with excitement. My daughter, sitting up high in the pack on my back hit my head with her little fists and squealed, "Bunny!" We were making memories for sure.

As we walked, I kept hearing a rattling noise coming from the grass that lined both sides of the trail and stretched as far as we could see. It sounded like there were a million rattlesnakes out there slithering right along with us on our hike. My five-year-old stopped and tilted his head.

"Mommy? Do you hear that? It sounds like there are a lot of rattlesnakes in that grass. Are there a lot of rattlesnakes in those grasses?"

"Oh, no, baby," I assured him, trying to keep that edge of anxiety out of my voice. "That sounds like too many rattlesnakes. It's impossible for there to be that many rattlesnakes, right? You know what I think it is? I think it's a bug that makes itself sound like a rattlesnake to trick all of its predators. It's smart, isn't it?"

"Oh, yeah," he said happily, now that the mystery was solved. "That's called camouflage."

The logical part of my brain believed those rattles were indeed coming from bugs hiding in the grass. But every time I heard the sound, my heart raced just a little bit. I tried to come up with a plan on the off chance that anyone got a rattlesnake bite. I wanted this adventure with my crew, but I was realizing adventuring came with a little more cost than our regular trips to the neighborhood park.

We walked on, the afternoon heat and the baby on my back making me sweat all over. My boys were oblivious, running ahead and then back to me, then darting off again. They didn't stay next to me, holding my hands, as I had imagined they would. But I didn't mind. That was for the grocery store and crossing the street. Here they could be free.

We rounded a curve in the trail, and my heart leapt into my throat. "Boys, stop!" I called, barely keeping the panic from my voice this time. They stopped in their tracks. I studied a dark shadow under a low-hanging branch of an oak tree, sure it was a mountain lion. The docent had warned me, but everything I knew about how to scare off a mountain lion flew out of my head in that split second. We just stood there, frozen, while my wildly beating heart took over my brain completely.

"Mommy!" my boys breathed in absolute delight. "It's a coyote! In the wild!"

Relief surged through me. My imagination had turned a medium-sized coyote into a big old mountain lion. My heart still raced, but my brain began to function again. I wasn't scared of the coyote. In fact, I was just as thrilled to see the creature as my kids were. He was beautiful. His presence felt like a gift to us, a way to turn this adventure into a memory we could hold onto forever. We stayed until the coyote disappeared into the brush. And then we turned around.

The sun was heading toward the mountaintops, and I surely was not going to be out on this trail at sunset. My longing for adventure and connection with my kids was superseded by my longing to stay alive. Or at least not to have any more heart-pounding moments.

It was a short hike. When I loaded my three kiddos into the car I didn't feel quite as confident or as enthusiastic as when I had set out. I hadn't done much at all. All we'd done was take a little walk down a trail. We hadn't gone far, and I'd been scared by fake rattlesnakes and a coyote. Here I was dreaming of having the sort of grand India adventures I'd had with my dad, but we couldn't even make it more than a mile down a trail at a nature preserve thirty minutes from my home. I longed for more. I longed to give them what my dad gave me.

The kids, though, had a totally different point of view.

"I can't wait to tell Daddy we saw a real live coyote!" my five-year-old said from the back seat.

"That was fun, Mommy," said the three-year-old. "Can we get ice cream now?"

PROVIDING A TRAINING GROUND

Beginning with the simpler and the smaller provides a training ground for bigger adventures to come. For example, from the time they're old enough to hike on their own two feet, I encourage my kids to carry their own backpacks. At first, their packs are small and light. They contain the bare essentials: a small water bottle and a few snacks. With time, though, they are able to carry more and more. By the time they're around eight or nine years old, they carry their own pack with adequate water for a long hike, plenty of snacks and lunch, and any other supplies they want to bring.

> Beginning with the simpler and the smaller provides a training ground for bigger adventures to come.

But, along the way, there's a learning curve. The responsibility, the growing, takes practice. And sometimes it's difficult. It seems to feel most difficult when we're hiking uphill, and even more when it's hot. That's when the inevitable question gets asked: "Will you carry my backpack for me?"

There are, of course, multiple ways to handle this seemingly simple question. Some parents avoid the problem altogether by not giving their kids packs to carry. The parents haul everything in their own backpacks. For me, this is not a practical solution. Just carrying enough water for my four kids and myself would cripple me. Not to mention the food, first aid kit, and other gear that keeps my pack stuffed full. Besides, I want my kids to learn to carry their own packs. It's a muscle they need to develop.

Other parents might solve the problem by responding with a quick, "Nope! You brought it, and you're responsible to carry it." The philosophy here is sound. These parents are training their kids to take care of themselves, especially when Mom or Dad isn't there to take the load for them. It's a good and worthy goal. But there is a part of me that struggles with this solution. Not because I disagree with the end goal. It is exactly what I want for my kids. I just prefer to take a different route to the same destination.

Why?

Well, to begin with, I want my kids to find hiking and adventuring so enjoyable that they're quick to say yes every time I suggest it. If it's drudgery for them each time we hike, they won't be excited to go. Then this opportunity to build heart connections becomes a struggle. Which is the opposite of what I am looking for in the short or long term.

Also, when we are hiking, I like to err on the side of

gentle. I want to encourage and help my kids. I want them to know they have my support on the trail and, indeed, in every part of their lives. I put myself in their shoes. If I were to ask my husband to carry my pack for a bit because I was worn out and he told me no, I'd be pretty crushed. If instead he offered to help me and give me a break, I would know I had the support I needed to continue.

So how do I accomplish these things while still training my kids to carry their own backpacks? To start with, when they ask me to carry their pack, I answer, "Sure, babe!" But then I add something else. "I'll set a timer for five minutes and carry it for that time. That way you can have a break. Then it will be your turn again." In this way my kids feel encouraged and supported. They also get a break if they're genuinely tired. Which does happen, especially when you're a little hiker. But then they get the responsibility brought back to them. It is the best of both worlds.

Sometimes, especially when the kids were really little, we traded packs every five minutes for the whole second half of a hike. But as each kid grew, they needed my help less and less. I can't recall the last time my older kids asked me to carry their backpacks for them, even when their packs were heavy, the trail was long, it was hot, and we were hiking uphill. Even then, they were able to carry their own load. Those small bits of help I offered them trained them for the harder hikes that lay ahead.

One day when my youngest was about seven, he asked for a backpack break. We were climbing the steepest part of a long hill, and all of us were tired. I obliged him, settling his pack onto my shoulder. "Thanks, Mom!" he called back as he quickly bounded up the hill, footloose and fancy-free. I couldn't help but smile at his obvious delight as I continued to trudge up the big hill, two backpacks now on my back. When the five minutes were done, I called for him to stop. He waited for me, and when I caught up, I handed the pack back to him. He carried it the rest of the hike. Those five minutes were all he needed from me. And they were not such a big price to pay to give him the support he needed.

In this "learning to carry your own pack" part of adventuring, things are at work on two different levels. On the surface level, my kids are learning personal responsibility, and they are training for bigger adventures yet to come. But on a deeper level, they are learning that they can do hard things. And when it gets so hard that they need some help from me, I am there to offer the support they need. If I had waited until my kids were all big enough and strong enough to carry their own packs for a whole hike, we'd have missed out on these small, but so impactful, lessons that they learned when their little legs carried them along the hiking trail.

BUILDING STRONG CONNECTIONS

Small adventures also build such strong connections. I love to think of these adventures as small but mighty. Oftentimes, it is not the size of the adventure that leaves the imprint on our hearts but the thought, time, and intention that went into it. When I was growing up, my family spent many summer Sunday afternoons at the beach. Sundays were the one day of the week my dad didn't have to work. We'd load up the van right after church and stay long after dark, wrapped up in warm sweatshirts or, more often, swimming in the waves by moonlight.

My mom always packed a cooler full of drinks and bags full of snacks. We'd have hot dogs or hamburgers cooked on our little hibachi grill. My brother and I spent hours in the water on boogie boards or inner tubes. My mom and dad took turns napping and watching us because they didn't fully trust that the lifeguards could watch all the people in the water. We dug deep holes in the sand, constructed tunnels, and made towering sandcastles. We took long walks to the ice cream shop down the beach. We looked for crabs in the rocks and caught sand crabs in the wet sand. Dad always came in to swim with us after he napped. He'd take us out deep, where the big waves were rougher and scarier. He showed us how to dive under big waves and body-surf the calmer ones. We were braver when he was with us. We lived out the spirit of adventure on those sandy summer days.

> It is not the size of the adventure that leaves the imprint on our hearts but the thought, time, and intention that went into it.

I look back with such fondness on those summer beach days. Our family didn't have much money when I was growing up, so those Sunday afternoons at the beach were kind of like our family vacations. We never took a trip to Europe together.

We didn't even travel by plane inside the United States. It just wasn't something we could swing on our budget. But the smallness and simplicity of our beach days didn't diminish the joy we experienced, the connections they created, or the memories that our family made on the sand and in the waves.

Those Sunday afternoon beach days made such a lasting impression on my heart that my husband and I made them a part of our own family life. Many Sunday afternoons of the summer you'll find us loading up the car with kayaks, a cooler, and sand toys. I'll fill the cooler with cold drinks and an unholy number of snacks, and then we'll head to our special beach.

We've been going for so many years now that the neighbors whose houses line the beach know our kids and comment at the start of every summer how much the kids grew over the winter. We park our stuff on the sand, and everyone gets down to serious play: swimming, sandcastle building, kayaking, and myriad other favorite beach activities. Friends are often at our beach, only adding to the fun. On the best days, the fireboat comes by, and the kids start chanting, "Spray us! Spray us!" Slowly the boat pulls closer to shore, and the crew crank open the nozzle on the deck of the boat and begin showering the waiting kids with cold seawater. They dance and scream in delight. Every time it happens, I hold the moment in my heart. What sweet memories we already have of those fireboat sprays.

As the sun starts to go down, we always eat dinner on the sand, sometimes picking up a pizza or burritos, sometimes bringing sandwiches from home. And on other evenings we plan a picnic with friends. The sunset always seems to be an especially gorgeous one, and the sunrays set the water aglow. We leave after dark, sandy and happy from another day spent together making the same memories that are somehow still special and remarkable every single time.

Because small adventures take less work to make happen, we're more likely to take them. That alone builds strong connections! We can't create bonds through adventures if we're never going on any. And though a small adventure might lack grand views or heart-stopping excitement, that just allows us to focus more on one another. The joy of the adventure is simply spending time together. We must not discount an adventure because it is small. Instead, we need to recognize that the act of being with one another, no matter the place or activity, is what really creates bonds that last.

MAKING THE MOST OF "SMALL"

Our "small" beach is actually a bay without big surf, and therefore perfect for our kids when they were little and not yet water safe. But as our kids have grown, we've figured out how to make our special beach grow with them. That way the smallness of it doesn't feel boring or childish. With each year they are given new freedom and the opportunity to explore and adventure on their own. As they become more accomplished swimmers, they can swim or kayak farther and farther out on the bay by themselves or with friends. It's a very big day when they are given the chance to swim all the way across the bay and then back again. Or sometimes they just like to kayak down the beach, looking for starfish and stingrays. The thrill is being given the freedom to explore on their own. It would be easy for our kids to view this stretch of beach as too small for them as they've gotten older. But by letting the adventures grow as they do, we're setting them up to learn how to have adventures wherever they are.

If we want to teach our kids contentment, we have to practice it ourselves. If we want to teach them to bloom where they are planted, and to make the most with what they've been given, we need to model that behavior for them. A big part of that is not waiting for the real adventures to happen but making whatever you are able to do right now the real adventure. If my parents had waited until they could take us to Hawaii on a "real" beach adventure, we would have missed out on all the joy and connection our "small" beach days brought us.

We live in a world that celebrates the big and the bold. Therefore, it is easy to fall prey to the idea that, unless our adventures are grandiose, they don't count. That just isn't true! No one starts off river rafting on Class 5 rapids. We all begin with a slow and easy Class 1 and build confidence and experience from there. If you really want to connect with your kids through adventure, just start where you are. Don't wait until you and your kids are ready for something you think is "big" enough. Small adventures count. Small adventures matter. Small adventures bring joy. Small adventures are the stepping stones to bigger ones.

Chapter 4

HOW TO CONTINUE

Be Intentional

We are what we repeatedly do. Excellence,
then, is not an act, but a habit.
—WILL DURANT

*O*ur kids are not the only ones who are busy and distracted in this day and age. Parents are too. Most of us
deal with the combination of busy schedules and the siren

call of technology every day. Therefore, we must be all the more diligent about carving out consistent time to adventure with our kids. Because connections aren't created by accident. Whether you are able to adventure together every week or every month, the thing that matters is that the adventures continue to happen again and again. This consistency builds a familiarity and comfort with both the adventuring and the time spent together, and it also creates a longing for the adventures to continue.

But oftentimes we fill up our schedules with things like soccer and football, going to practices on weeknights and games on the weekends. Our days and nights are so full and busy. We're together, yet not. Our kids are spending much more time connecting and making memories with the kids on their teams than with their parents. I know it is countercultural to say so, but maybe it's time we stepped back and made building connections in our families our number one priority.

These are some of the considerations that led our family to pursue other ways of spending our time. We recognized we couldn't shuttle our four kids to four different sports or other classes and activities. We had to minimize our activities with other people and maximize our time together. So many parents see sports, lessons, classes, and extracurricular activities as nonnegotiable. They don't even question spending massive amounts of time running their kids from practices to games to more practices to classes. I wonder if they even know there is an alternative.

Sometimes when people hear that we choose connection over activities they question us about the "wasted" time. Just because the outcome of an adventure is not measurable does not mean it is wasted time. True, there are no trophies or awards ceremonies. And you might not see the positive outcomes of your adventures for years to come. But that isn't why we're doing this. We're chasing adventure with our kids to build relationship for the many years ahead.

When I first began adventuring with my kids, I really had no idea what I was doing. I didn't have a big plan or a bunch of research to justify what I felt. I just had a longing in my heart to get my little kids outside the four walls of our home, away from the call of chores for me and toys for them. Our schedules weren't packed with T-ball or classes yet. But still, I knew now was the time to start consciously building connection between us. I knew I needed to be intentional about this from the beginning.

> **Just because the outcome of an adventure is not measurable does not mean it is wasted time.**

I thought of the things that filled me and listened. My soul longed for fresh air, nature, and room for my boys to run. As a stay-at-home mom of young kids, I wanted to explore and see new places, even if it just meant heading to the very next town. And I wanted to introduce my kids to the joy of discovery and the delight of wondering what was waiting for us around the bend. More than anything, I wanted to be with my kids in a way that invited connection and memory-making. Recalling my own childhood, I knew a surefire way to build connection was to get away from our everyday world and routine to do something new. One day I decided it was time. I loaded everyone in the minivan, and we headed out in search of our first adventure together.

In the years that followed, adventuring together became a regular part of our life. We adventured on our own or with friends every week and planned our school schedule and other activities around these outings. I know some people find the thought of this overwhelming. I know all that planning and then actually going on so many adventures can feel like too much. But the vast majority of our adventures were easy to take and pretty close to home. Most of the time, they weren't anything spectacular. They just elevated our day-to-day life a little bit. It wasn't so much about what we did or where we were but that we made a point of being together, week after week. That's what made the impact.

Of course, I listened to my kids, too, learning their favorite hikes or other places to visit. I made sure the adventures weren't just filling my tank but theirs as well. It's easy to know the things that fill me up and bring me joy. But providing adventures for my kids that fill them up, too, has required years of spending time with them and studying who they are.

I want to know my kids in an intimate way. I want to know the things that delight them and scare them, the things they'd like to learn more about and the things that they used to love but have moved on from. By knowing them this way I can be sure that our time spent adventuring is purposeful in reaching my goal, and I'm not simply checking it off the list of things that has to be done this week. Creating connection and strengthening our relationship is the driving force behind all of our adventures.

INTENTIONAL PLANNING

My oldest was only five when we began taking these weekly adventures. Small, doable adventures were key to making sure they happened over and over again. The kids were easy to please at that age; practically anything could be an adventure. But as they grew older and we kept on adventuring, I didn't want the adventures to become routine or stale. I wanted to make sure the way we spent our time still appealed to their hearts, making them feel known and seen. So, my adventure planning became even more strategic and thoughtful, and sometimes we took on bigger adventures—ones that were farther from home and farther outside our comfort zone.

One spring day I gave the kids a packing list and said, "I need you to pack a bag. We're going on a trip tomorrow."

They were immediately full of questions: "What kind of trip? Where? Are we staying in a hotel? Are we camping? Is Daddy coming? Are our friends coming? Is it far away?"

I answered a few of their questions but intentionally didn't answer all of them. It was so fun to let them wonder.

Later that day, the kids helped me pull some of our camping gear from the garage and load it in the car.

"We're packing the camping stove but not the tent . . . hmm. This is very mysterious." I could hear them talking all afternoon, speculating and wondering and guessing.

All I would say was, "We're going on an adventure. I know you, and I know what you love. You can trust me. It's going to be great!" They knew I was right, so they let it rest.

This trip was a spur-of-the-moment decision. We'd been in an extra busy season of life, and I wanted time away to connect with my kids. I knew we all needed it. Feeling that tug in my heart, I searched online, found a private camping site a few hours from home, and booked it. It was in a place I'd never been to, or even heard of, camping on a stranger's property, and, to be honest, I felt a teensy bit nervous. This was definitely outside my comfort zone. I told a few friends where we were going and gave them the address and phone number, since I wouldn't have cell service. "Come look for us if you don't hear from us in a few days," I told them, mostly joking.

The next morning, we set out. My husband was out of town for work, so it was just me and the kids. We drove north along the coast, a route familiar to all of us. Which of course led to more speculation. "If this is the way, I know where we're going!" they all said at one point or another. But when I turned off the freeway and began driving away from the ocean and toward the mountains, they no longer knew the route and just had to sit back and see what I had planned for them.

We stopped in a new town to look for ice cream, coffee,

and a bookstore, because those are our essentials on a road trip. We found a fun playground where the six-year-old could stretch his legs and we all could laugh and play together, spinning on the merry-go-round and flying through the air on the giant tire swing. As long as I've had littles, playground stops have also been an essential part of road trips. It's important to know what helps each kid get through a long drive with a smile on his face. Once we'd had a good break, I filled up the gas tank, not sure where the next gas station would be, and we drove off into the mountains.

"I've never been where we're going," I confessed to the kids as the road wound up the mountainside and we climbed higher and higher. "But I'm excited!"

There is nothing quite like sharing a new experience to build instant connection. Every time the view opened up around another bend in the road, we all gasped and called out to each other, "Oh, wow! Did you see that?" We were lost in the moment together. It was just what I had hoped for.

When we crested the mountain, the topography changed, and the exclamations changed too: "Look at the pine trees!" "It feels like we're on Big Thunder Mountain!" "Look how red the rocks are!" "It doesn't even feel like we're in California anymore!" We hadn't even reached our destination yet, and already we were totally removed from our everyday life, being doused in the joy and excitement of discovery. *This is why we do this*, I thought. *It's worth every bit of effort and planning.*

A couple hours later I pulled off the two-lane highway

onto a dusty dirt road. We were in the high desert, so the pine trees were gone and the mountains were covered with low shrubs. Since it was early spring, the sun hadn't yet burnt off the wildflowers or the green fuzz on the hills. The only sign of human life was one rambling house and barn at the end of the road.

"Where are we?" the kids wondered.

"I don't really know," I replied as we bumped down the road to the house.

No one answered when I knocked on the door, but there was a note pinned to it telling me where to go. So I got back in the car and drove farther down the road.

"We're not staying at the house?" the kids asked in surprise. "Mom! Where are we going?"

I couldn't help laughing as I replied in a singsong voice, "Wait and see!"

That's when we turned a corner and my oldest yelled, "Is that a tepee? We're staying in a tepee?" And then they all just went crazy with excitement.

We'd been camping many times but had never stayed in a tent quite like this one. It was a giant canvas tepee, big enough to fit all of us inside comfortably. There were rugs on the floor and comfy mattresses to stretch out on, and there was a trunk full of warm quilts and soft pillows.

"You guys!" I called to them excitedly as they rolled around the floor of the tepee like a pack of puppies. "We're going glamping! What do you think?" They all kind of tackled me in a giant hug, a physical representation of their delight at such an unexpected kind of adventure. It was so perfect I cried.

The tepee was nestled at the foot of a big hill, with nothing around it except a fire ring, a picnic table, and, down the hill a ways, a rustic wooden outhouse. At night the stars lit up the sky, and all we could hear was the coyotes howling. We hung out in our comfy tepee, playing card games, having a glow-stick dance party, and telling stories.

It was intimate and felt so special, even though it wasn't all that different from spending the night together in our regular tent. Intentionally doing something outside our normal life, and even outside our normal adventures, brought my kids an extra measure of delight.

SETTING ASIDE TIME ON PURPOSE

It's easy to think that just spending time together is enough to fill our kids' hearts and create connections. As a homeschooler, I should have it easy, right? I'm with my kids all the time. Early on, though, it became clear to me that I could not count on building connections with my kids simply because they were home with me daily. There still had to be thoughtful, intentional activities that connected their hearts and mine.

I also knew that establishing adventures as a consistent routine and habit while they were young would make it so much easier to continue adventuring when they were older.

Now, ten years after we began, I can say that's true. The distractions, obligations, and activities at home or in our daily lives create such a loud chorus that sometimes I can't hear the voices of my children. If I'm not careful, I don't really look in their eyes through the day. I can take them places and not engage with them in the activities we do there. I am busy. They are busy. And living life at that pace, it would be easy for us to let a week or even a month slip past without really stopping and letting our hearts connect. But by intentionally setting aside time to adventure for all these years, we've made sure that doesn't happen.

Consistently choosing to adventure with our kids, outside of our regular routine, requires special commitment.

I know we're not the only family living in the midst of distraction and full schedules. I know that this kind of fractured family life is an epidemic all over America. But I'm here to remind you that we don't have to throw our hands in the air with despair and give up. This disconnectedness does not have to be our fate. Instead, we can choose something different. We can create lasting connections with our kids by choosing them over and over again.

It's easy to choose them every now and then on a special trip or to say we're spending purposeful time together doing things that already exist in our life, like church, music lessons, or sports practices. But consistently choosing to adventure with our kids, outside of our regular routine, requires special commitment. Really, it's what every parent longs for in this busy, distracted world we live in—a space and place to carve out time together. We can't just expect this to happen. We have to make the space and the place for connections to grow, over and over again.

Chapter 5

HOW TO THRIVE

Grow Your Adventures

Be not afraid of growing slowly, be afraid only of standing still.
—CHINESE PROVERB

"Tell us a story, Daddy," my brother and I begged nearly every night before we went to bed. We could think of no better way to drift off to dreamland than by hearing tales of our dad's boyhood escapades and adventures. He had so many wildly fun, interesting, and exciting stories, and we never, ever tired of hearing them.

One story in particular always stood out to me, and I asked to hear it more than once. It was from when my dad was a young man, only twenty or twenty-one years old. He and a few of his buddies drove high into the Sierra Nevada; strapped on backpacks loaded with canned food, sleeping bags, and a tent; and headed out in search of beauty and adventure.

My dad would tell us about the whole trip, highlighting the parts that still stood out to him all those years later. He told us how crystal clear the water was when he dove into an icy mountain lake. "You can't even imagine it, guys! You could see every stone on the bottom. It was incredible!" He told us that the water was so cold it took his breath away, and he came up spluttering and yelling because it felt like his skin was on fire from the freezing water. We'd howl with delight when he'd demonstrate for us what he looked like, yelling, slapping his arms and chest, and shivering dramatically.

He told us about the sky, so dark at night and lit up by millions of the brightest stars he'd ever seen. There were brilliant green alpine meadows and snowcapped peaks. There were giant sequoia trees. And miles and miles of rough and rocky trails to hike with no one else out there but bears, deer, and maybe even some mountain lions. As he talked, I could hear the wonder and delight in his voice. That trip still filled him up. It had changed him. And my little-girl heart longed for the very same experience.

Oh, how I wanted to go on a backpacking trip! To me, backpacking seemed like the height of adventure. Sleeping in the great outdoors in places only accessible by your own two feet—magic. I wanted to see those crystal-clear waters, those alpine meadows, and maybe even a bear. Those stories planted a seed of a dream deep in my heart, and I began to ask, "Daddy, when can we go on a backpacking trip?"

His answer was always the same: "I want to, honey. Maybe one day we can." But that day didn't come. Backpacking trips require a fair amount of gear. Which costs money. And they require preparation. Which takes time. There is also the time required to actually go on the trip. Time and money were in pretty short supply around our home when I was a girl. Thus, the backpacking trip I longed for never materialized.

Years later, I was an adult, but I still hadn't gone on that backpacking trip. And I still wanted to. Badly. One summer my mother-in-law told me she was going on a backpacking trip in Yosemite National Park with a group of girlfriends. "How amazing that will be!" I exclaimed, delighted for her. And, I admit, a touch envious.

"Why don't you come?" she invited me. "You'll need your own pack and gear, some good shoes, and to carry your own food and water."

I jumped at the chance. And immediately began to dream about the backpacking trip I'd been hoping for since girlhood finally coming true. But backpacking trips didn't seem like they were in the cards for me. My husband and I were young newlyweds on a tight budget. Buying all the gear I'd need for the trip just wasn't feasible.

My young husband also wasn't totally on board with me traipsing out into the wilderness. Even though I was going with his mom. He worried I might cause my old back injury to flare up by carrying a heavy pack, and then how would I get back to civilization? He worried about bears and my body's allergic reaction to mosquitos. He worried that I was being too ambitious for my first ever backpacking trip. He and I had experienced a lot of really amazing adventures together. But letting go and letting me grow as an adventurer on my own was scary for him. Growth is not always easy.

CHALLENGING YOUR KIDS AND YOURSELF

Growth is a critical part of life. Without it there is a shrinking, and, eventually, there is death. When we begin adventuring with our kids, it is all new. Being beginners, we start with the small, manageable adventures and build our confidence. The temptation, of course, is to never move beyond those small adventures. We get comfortable. Trouble is, those comfortable adventures will eventually become stale and boring. Then our kids will no longer want to join us; their phones, friends, activities, or video games will be more exciting than the walks through the nature center they've done with us so many times.

As our kids grow and as our own confidence grows, our adventures need to grow too. Experiencing new places and things keeps adventuring fresh and exciting. We never want our adventures to become just another chore to check off our list.

This doesn't mean you have to train for a wilderness survival expedition—unless you want to. It just means that your family might try an overnight camping trip for the first time—in the woods or in your backyard. Or a trip to a real art museum instead of a children's museum. Growing your adventures means pushing your kids and yourself to try things that challenge you all. Those challenges will draw you together and forge those heart connections that you long to create ever stronger.

> We never want our adventures to become just another chore to check off our list.

I have always been ready to jump into new adventures. This kind of growth doesn't scare me. It is essential to my emotional well-being. I married a man, however, who is far more cautious and thoughtful than I am. He wants a plan and to weigh the options before we jump in. I appreciate his steady ways, because my wild personality needs some steadiness added to it. But Aaron needs some of my wild too. He needs to be pushed to say yes to growth and to jumping into the unknown when comfortable sounds so much better. Quite honestly, it has taken us many years to find a healthy, happy balance between my wild and his steady. The growth hasn't always been easy. But as we've fought for it, we've blossomed and, best of all, surprised ourselves with what we're capable of.

Meanwhile, I still hadn't gone on that backpacking trip.

The backpacking trip to Yosemite didn't happen. The years passed, and I kept dreaming. One of the issues with my being a dreamer is I dream big. I had so built up this backpacking trip in my mind since girlhood that, if it was anything less than incredible, I just couldn't see it counting. I'm afraid I missed out on a lot of growth as a result.

You see, we could have taken an overnight backpacking trip in the mountains forty-five minutes from our home. But that didn't seem like enough to me. I wanted to drive hours, hike at eleven thousand feet, and feel like a wild adventurer. So I just kept waiting for that one day to come, when in actuality nothing was happening at all.

Except for babies. Lots of babies were happening. Which made the idea of a backpacking trip feel farther away than ever. You know how hard it is to get away for even one night when you have little ones. And if you do somehow, magically, get a night away from your house full of little people, a comfy bed and room service sound better than a sleeping bag, a tiny backpacking tent, and freeze-dried meals eaten out of a tin cup. A part of me was ready to give up on the dream forever. Our adventures were growing in lots of other ways. Backpacking wasn't the be-all and end-all.

Still, despite trying to talk myself out of it, I couldn't quite shake the idea of a real adventurous destination. The dream persisted. And, eventually, my backpacking dream did come true! My sure and steady husband helped me make that dream become reality. He helped us grow. Not in the way I'd imagined. But, in the end, it was better.

ALWAYS ROOM FOR MORE GROWTH

"Hey! Why don't we all go backpacking this weekend?" Aaron texted me from work one Thursday afternoon.

"Really?" I texted back, feeling a little dubious. "Like in two days? All of us? Davy too?"

"Yes!" Aaron responded. "We can figure out gear we need tonight and rent a tent from REI. The trail to the campsite isn't that long. Davy can do it."

And just like that, the same guy who had been too worried to let his twenty-four-year-old wife go backpacking with his mom was suggesting we take our four kids backpacking with only a day and a half to prepare. What was happening? Now I was the one with concerns. I was the one holding back, feeling worried about getting outside my comfort zone. I was the one afraid to grow. Because this adventure was for sure going to bring some growth.

First of all, our kids had never been part of my backpacking dream. I mean, I wanted to backpack with them eventually, but not on my first trip. And this destination wasn't what I had in mind either. Only a couple hours from home. Was that really far enough? But my real concerns were what tempted me to cancel this trip. Could our seven-year-old carry a backpack up a mountainside? And could we make up the difference of what he couldn't carry in our packs? What would we feed everyone? Especially that seven-year-old? Would the six of us fit in two small backpacking tents? Would we freeze at night? Were we really going on a family backpacking trip?

But Aaron assured me we could do it. "It's only one night," he said. "We'll all survive."

He was right. But we didn't just survive. We thrived. Even though nothing went according to plan.

A car accident on the two-lane mountain road shut it down for hours, so we didn't arrive at the trailhead until the early afternoon. Because of the time of day, it was hot when we set out, walking straight uphill and with no forest canopy to provide shade. As anticipated, the seven-year-old dragged his feet. He dragged his whole body. His pack was heavy. And he was right. It was the heaviest pack he'd had to carry on a hike yet. He was hot. Right again. It was hot. We were all hot. The trail was steep. It was so steep. At one point early on, he sat down on the trail and started crying, saying he didn't want to go on. I kind of wanted to sit down and cry too. This wasn't the dream trip I'd had in my mind all these years. It was nothing like the rugged, romantic beauty my dad conveyed in his stories of hiking the Sierra Nevadas.

Oh, it's so hard to grow sometimes, isn't it? This backpacking trip really was about different kinds of growth happening in all of us. First, my own dream had to grow. It had to grow to include my family. And for me to see that it didn't have to be all or nothing. It could just be different. For my husband, growth was the recognition that now, almost twenty years later, his wife could carry a backpack up a hill and not injure her back. The years had given him time to see my growth as a strong, capable woman, and time for him to let go of worry and the fear of discomfort.

And then there were the kids. Their growth was remarkable! When we first began hiking together, my oldest was five. I never imagined we'd all be going on an overnight backpacking trip together in a few years. That was in the distant future, I was sure. But my kids had built up stamina, endurance, and confidence from hiking every week. I was so proud to see the way all three of my older kids shouldered their packs and marched up that hill like it was nothing. In fact, the minute we got to our campsite and heaved our packs from our shoulders, Lilly sighed happily and said, "I can't wait to do this again!" They enjoyed the climb, stopping to admire the view and getting far enough ahead to turn around and encourage us to catch up and see the next cool thing. They had definitely grown far beyond those first hikes in the nature center.

Davy, our youngest and most reluctant backpacker, still had a lot of room to grow. But, in comparison to his siblings at this age, he'd already come pretty far. I would never have dreamed of taking them backpacking at age seven. But Davy had been on the hiking trail since he was six weeks old. As soon as he could walk, he'd cry to get out of the carrier and hike the trail on his little unsteady feet. He was hiking miles by age three or four, sometimes carrying his own backpack and other times handing it off to me. He'd grown up on the trail. Adventuring was just a part of his life.

All of this said, his response to carrying his own heavy pack, without the option of someone carrying it for him, even for five minutes, was evidence that he wasn't done growing. No matter how far along we are on the journey, there is still always room for growth, isn't there? So, I handed Davy a lollipop, walked alongside him up the hill, sometimes at a snail's pace, and encouraged him to not give up. Not the free and easy backpacking trip of my dreams by any stretch of the imagination. But growth for both of us.

> No matter how far along we are on the journey, there is still always room for growth, isn't there?

Two miles doesn't sound like that long of a hike, unless its uphill the whole way at eight thousand feet, where it's harder to fill your lungs with air. Then those two miles are a lot harder. When we reached the top of the hill, our hearts stopped pumping so hard and our legs stopped burning. The views of pine tree–covered mountains transitioning into empty, sand-colored desert stretched out before us. It was beautiful. The sun sank lower, the air cooled, and while the kids figured out how to set up the tents, we filled our bottles with cool water from the spring.

Cooking dinner wasn't without its challenges. It takes a lot of water to rehydrate freeze-dried meals for six. And our one tiny backpacking stove had a single blue flame to heat one small pot of water after another. As the night went on, we made mental lists of all the things we'd do differently next time. An extra stove, less clothes, different food, bug spray, and, after the worst night's sleep ever, a better sleeping pad. There was room for growth. And dreams of the next trip to come.

In the end, my first backpacking trip was wonderful. Instead of a trip on my own, it was a whole family backpacking trip with the hope of so many more to come. It came with the knowledge that we could do something that seemed a little bit crazy and a little bit hard, a little bit outside our comfort zone. I loved that my original dream had been replaced with something better than I could have imagined. Never would I have dreamed that I'd be backpacking with my whole family! It was harder than I thought it would be, even though it was just one night. But that left room for us to grow and try something bigger and better.

Growing your adventures means trying things that challenge you all. Real growth means saying yes, even if it's hard or scary or new.

Those challenges will draw you together and those heart connections will be forged ever stronger.

Part 3

STEP INTO
ADVENTURE

Chapter 6

ADJUST YOUR ATTITUDE

Adventures are not all pony-rides in May-sunshine.
—J. R. R. TOLKIEN

*T*here were signs everywhere. Beware of Bears. We should leave no food in our car, not even a stray mint or scented sunscreen. The bears would smell it and pull the car door right off. All the photographs at the ranger station warned of it. I frantically searched our car with a flashlight, trying to find all the french fries, M&M's, and gum wrappers hiding under seats. After spending eight hours in the car, there were sure to be plenty.

"Car's all clean," I finally called to Aaron. He was pulling the last of our luggage out of the back of the minivan. The kids all stood around, their arms full of sleeping bags, pillows, and stuffed duffels. I carried a big bag of food and was only slightly worried a bear would sniff it from afar, come bursting out of the woods and into the parking lot, and snatch the bagels, avocados, and oranges right out of my arms.

Aaron got a better grip on the heavy cooler. "Let's go," he said, leading the way.

It was our first time visiting Yosemite National Park. We arrived long after dark, because rain and mudslides had caused freeway closures and long waits in traffic on our drive up. There were no stars to help light the path. The sky was heavy with clouds, and the air was bitter cold. I was so glad I had paid extra for a tent cabin with a heater. We'd never had such fancy camping accommodations. Before the night was over, I was even gladder we'd left our regular tent at home and decided to do this trip glamping-style.

We secured our food in the bear box right outside our tent, and I made sure no one had left any food in a jacket pocket or stuffed in the bottom of a backpack. Those tent cabin walls might have been thicker than a regular tent, but I was certain a bear could rip right through them if he caught a whiff of someone's bag of crushed potato chips. We piled blankets on top of sleeping bags, turned the heater on high, and settled down for our first night in the beautiful Yosemite Valley.

A crack rang through the darkness, like a rifle being shot right inside. Almost instantly our tent lit up as if we had turned on the single light bulb. Then the rain hit the canvas roof with such force we were sure it would fall in on us immediately. Another rifle shot. The claps of thunder seemed to bounce from one mountain to another, making an endless echo so that it felt like the very ground was shaking.

We'd never experienced anything like this before. Growing up in Southern California, our kids had experienced only a handful of thunderstorms. And even though Aaron and I had braved wild storms in Florida and Scotland (in tents even), this was a whole new level of intensity. The kids were scared. I was even a little scared. Aaron seemed calm and assured us we'd be fine. We huddled together, prayed for safety, and then crawled back in our sleeping bags and tried to sleep. Which was nearly impossible.

For what felt like hours, the thunder, lightning, and pouring rain kept up. Time passed, and my bladder let me know it needed to be emptied. But there was no way I was going to the bathrooms in that storm. The tent didn't feel very safe at the moment, but it sure felt safer than being outside. I decided I'd hold it. Until I couldn't hold it any longer. Then I did what anyone would do in the same situation. I peed in a trash can.

"Mom! What are you doing?" one of my sons whispered through the darkness.

"Shhh," I whispered back. "I'm peeing in the trash can. It's an emergency!"

"What?!" he shout-whispered. I could hear the incredulousness in his voice.

"It's okay," I told him. "There's a trash bag. We'll empty it in the morning. Just go back to sleep."

Finally feeling relief, I got back on my cot and listened to the rain fall. The thunder was still just as loud, but the measured breathing around our little tent told me that most of my family was asleep. I couldn't sleep. I just prayed that there would be no mudslides coming down a nearby mountain onto our tent, that the river wouldn't rise too high, that we wouldn't be struck by lightning, and that there would be no flash floods. The vision I'd had for our first family trip to Yosemite had been a lot more like Maria von Trapp twirling through a meadow than me being sleeplessly anxious about any number of impending weather-related disasters. At least I didn't have to worry about bears anymore.

WHEN THINGS GO WRONG

One of the most important things to remember when we're adventuring with our kids is that things will go wrong. But when plans go awry, or even straight-up failures happen, that is no reason to quit. Misadventures provide opportunity for both parents and kids to practice grace under pressure. We learn to make the best of things. Having a good attitude in these moments is everything.

This never proved truer than on that first morning after

the storm, when we woke up in Yosemite. I had been dreaming of this trip since I was ten years old. That was the one time I had been to Yosemite, and I had waited all those years to return. None of my family had ever been, and I wanted our few days there to be incredible. The bitter cold, the muddy, sodden ground, and the pouring rain were not part of my plans or my dreams. I can assure you, there was nothing *Sound of Music–*like on that gray morning.

October is usually a month of glorious weather in California. So this storm caught us by surprise. Thankfully, I had packed some warm clothes and had made a last-minute purchase of cheap rain ponchos from Target. We bundled up in all the layers, strapped on backpacks, and put those flimsy ponchos on over it all. Outside our tent the air was cold. We could see our breath but none of the beautiful mountains that ringed the valley. We tried to avoid the puddles and the mud, but since we hadn't come with rain boots, our sneakers were soon soaked through. We stood shivering and wet, waiting for the bus to take us to the visitor center to see if there were any trails we could hike after the epic downpour. My attitude was sinking just like our shoes in the mud. I was so mad at how our trip was turning out.

We boarded the bus and immediately began to sweat. The heat was on, and our plastic ponchos trapped it all in. Our extra layers of clothing didn't help. We were legitimately

> Misadventures provide opportunity for both parents and kids to practice grace under pressure.

uncomfortable. The kids started to complain and grumble, and I did too. I just didn't have it in me to encourage anyone to look on the bright side, choose joy, or trust that we'd still have fun. I wanted to wallow in vacation-gone-wrong blues.

It started pouring again, a torrential downpour like the night before. When the bus stopped near the visitor center, we stepped right into it. Those ponchos provided next to no protection. We were getting soaked. And I was fuming inside. I wanted to have a temper tantrum. To stamp my feet in every puddle and shake my fist at God, "This isn't fair!" And, to be honest, as we ran through the rain, I was pretty much doing just that.

What would we do for the next two days? Sit inside our little canvas tent? We didn't have the right rain gear for spending time outside in the rain or cold. I kicked the puddles and didn't even try to pretend I wasn't mad.

The visitor center was crawling with people. We were all trying to escape the downpour. The kids explored the cool displays about the park, and we tried to figure out what we could see in the rain and what we could see if it ever stopped. Eventually, we opted to watch a movie about the park. As we settled into our seats, stuffing wet ponchos and coats and backpacks under the seats in front of us and listening to the kids complain they were hungry, I tried to quiet the angry voices in my head and heart.

The movie about Yosemite's history was so inspiring. I found myself loving the park even more but then being near tears to think we wouldn't get to experience so much of it.

The rain was still falling when the movie ended, but my husband said he had a plan. "We're getting back on the bus," he told me. "And we're going to check out the Ahwahnee hotel."

It wasn't ideal, I thought to myself, but what other choices did we have? At least we could walk around inside and not be soaked. It would have been nice if I could have been grateful for the buses to ride from place to place. For sleeping in a waterproof tent with a heater that was on a raised platform off the ground, keeping us from getting flooded in the night. But I didn't want to. I chose to wallow. Which we sometimes do, right? I didn't hide it from my kids. I was the captain of complaining. I knew I was wrecking our time. But I didn't even care.

We walked into the big, beautiful Ahwahnee hotel, crowded with fellow campers trying to escape the rain. There were fireplaces big enough to stand in, piled high with logs and throwing out comforting heat. Huge beams spanned the tall ceilings, and gorgeous details hid round every corner. I could feel the years of campers who had filled this place. This was the Yosemite of my dreams. I felt my anger begin to melt just a little. And then my sweet husband jumped in to save the day.

"Come this way, guys!" he called to us from across one of the big public rooms.

We made our way toward him. "What are we doing?" we all wanted to know.

He grinned at us. "We're having lunch in the dining room!"

"What?" I gasped. "But it's expensive! We didn't plan for that. I have lunch stuff back in the bear box."

Aaron brushed my protestations aside. "We can eat that for dinner."

"But it's so fancy. Look at us! We're a mess! We can't, Aaron."

He looked me in the eye and smiled but said seriously, "We need this right now. It's beautiful in there. Come see."

And, just like that, the tides of our adventure gone wrong began to turn.

I gasped when we walked into the dining room. The beamed ceiling stretched high overhead. The room was incredibly spacious and so beautiful. It felt every bit like the grand dining room it was meant to be. The big windows opening onto a meadow behind the ballroom utterly captured my heart. Even with the rain streaming down, the views were breathtaking. I imagined sitting there in the winter, with glittering white snow covering everything. Or in the springtime, when there were brightly colored wildflowers and green grasses and trees budding out with fresh green leaves. My imagination flew to the next adventures—we'd be back to visit this spot in all those seasons. The skies were still dark, but the day had brightened completely.

Our kind waiter brought hot cocoa and fries for the kids. Aaron and I sipped hot coffee and had bowls of warm soup. Our wild and tired two-year-old fell asleep with his head in my lap, his body stretched across two dining room chairs. We were warm and dry and oh so comfortable. Everyone's mood lifted, and naturally we began to talk about the big storm the night before.

"It was *so* loud!"

"I was a little bit scared!"

"Did you know Mom peed in the trash can?"

"I never saw lightning like that!"

"I'm so glad we got to be in that storm. It was *so* cool!"

Already the storm had become an epic adventure and part of our family history. It bound us together in a way that a calm, quiet, and dry night never would have. That is the magic of misadventure. The hardships and the struggle, the scary parts, even the undesirable parts all create this special bond that happens faster and holds stronger than the bonds made in our regular humdrum days. The humdrum days are important too. We have to keep showing up for those. But we shouldn't consider all to be loss when the misadventure happens. We should hold on with all our might, pray for a good attitude, ask for forgiveness when we've lost it, and remind ourselves of this important fact: it will make a good story later.

I have shared this truth with my kids for years now. Every time things fall apart on an adventure, or at the very least don't go as we planned, I say one of our family mottos: "It will make a good story later." For someone who makes big plans and wants nothing more than to see them worked out perfectly, this is such an important motto to live by. And on the days when I am collapsing into a bad attitude because everything is going wrong and I just don't have the strength to be positive, God sends helpers my way. Sometimes my husband comes to the rescue. But more often than not, it's my kids. With gentleness they'll come alongside me and offer a hug and some sweet encouragement. "It will be okay, Mom. Really. We can still have fun. And besides, it will make a great story later."

And there we were, living out that motto in the heart of the Yosemite Valley after a freak fall rainstorm, with more rain being dumped on the park than had been for months. We didn't even know the half of the great stories to be told from the rest of our trip. We were already so happy about the one we'd lived to tell about from the night before.

REDEMPTION AT WORK

After our long and leisurely lunch, which totally destroyed my careful plans to see as much of the park as possible in three short days, the rain stopped. We didn't know for how long, but we sure weren't going to waste it. We walked out into the valley for an easy hike. The giant rocks and peaks surrounding Yosemite were still covered by low-hanging clouds, and any of the more famous, and difficult, hikes were too muddy and treacherous for our crew of small hikers, but our mood was lifted. We exclaimed over the full river running through the valley, the roar of waterfalls, and the beauty of the wet and soggy meadow. It was nothing that we had planned for, yet it was somehow just right.

That night, snuggled in our warm, dry tent, I made sure to apologize to everyone for my bad attitude. I told them I knew they saw me being angry and disappointed and not handling it like I should. I wanted this trip to be the best, and all I saw was everything going wrong. It felt like too much to bear, and I stopped trying. "I needed help," I told them. "I couldn't do it myself. And that's when Daddy did help." Aaron had come up with a plan and invited me into it. In the kindest and gentlest of ways, he asked me to try to change my outlook. And when I did, everything was so much better.

What a lesson that was to share with our kids. That adventures—and really life, right?—are not always fun. Over the years of adventuring with my kids, I've learned that someone is always unhappy, tired, bored, hungry, sick, mad, grumpy, frustrated, or disappointed. As much as I want everyone happy all the time, that just doesn't happen. I mean, *I'm* not happy all the time. But those times of bad attitudes in the face of misadventure are such an opportunity to extend grace to one another. And to see redemption at work. Not just the redemption of a bad situation being turned into something wonderful. Although that is really powerful. But the redemption of a heart being changed. That is something even more powerful.

Our kids need to see and hear us experiencing these things. They need to know that they aren't the only ones who struggle with anger, disappointment, and frustration. Moms and dads feel those things too! And sometimes they handle them just like little kids do. Cue the parent temper tantrum. But in those moments, we invite God into the misadventure. And just like he changed the story for the whole world, he can change your story too.

That next morning, we saw redemption at work. The rainstorm brought unimaginable beauty to the valley that wouldn't have happened otherwise. I woke my two oldest boys up for an early morning walk in the meadow near our tent. We stopped for hot cocoa to try to combat some of the chill of a very cold morning. When we walked out of the forest surrounding the campground and the views opened up around us, we all gasped in unison. The clouds were gone, and we could finally see the grandeur of the rocky peaks that surrounded this special place. Tumbling down from the rocks ringing the valley were so many small and magical waterfalls. The roar of the large ones could be heard from far away, but it was these small ones that captured our hearts utterly.

> Invite God into the misadventure. And just like he changed the story for the whole world, he can change your story too.

"There's one!" the boys called eagerly.

"And another one!"

"I see two more!"

They were everywhere, and they were just glorious. It was unlike anything we'd ever seen before. We learned later that these kinds of waterfalls are called "ephemeral" waterfalls. They occur usually only in winter and early spring, fed by large rains or snow melt. These waterfalls are rare at any time of year, but especially in early fall. Some last a few weeks, some only a day. That we got to experience that phenomenon felt like a true gift to my heart after such a rough first day. Did I deserve that gift after such a childish reaction to my plans being changed? No, I did not. But that's just the way grace works, isn't it? We'll never forget the sight of those waterfalls cascading down the granite walls of Yosemite. But even more, we'll never forget the lessons they taught us.

What do you do when adventures don't go as planned? Here are some ideas to get you started!

Stop and pray.

Even, and especially when, we don't feel like it, prayer is important, because it resets our hearts and reminds us that we're not in control, but God is.

If we're scared, God assures us.

If we're angry, God quiets us.

If we're frustrated, God calms us.

Pray for one another.

There have been times in the middle of an adventure gone wrong when one of my kids has said, "Mommy, should we pray?" And I honestly don't feel like praying in the moment. I'll ask them to pray instead. When they do, every time,

I feel a sense of peace wash over me. Inviting our kids into our moments of weakness allows them to be used by God to help the family. That's an incredible gift for all of us.

Practice reframing.

This is a very important practice in our family, one I start teaching my kids from the time they're toddlers. Reframing is choosing to look for the good in a situation where it's hard to find. It's often called looking on the bright side or seeing the silver lining. Reframing doesn't mean we dismiss hardship or trouble. We can acknowledge the situation is not what we wished for, but then we state there is still something about it that will bring good. One of my greatest joys as a parent is seeing my children take up this practice on their own. Especially when I'm struggling to reframe and they step in and help me.

Practice flexibility.

A great life skill to pass onto our children is the art of flexibility. If they can bend when the wind blows rather than break, their lives will be better. Adventures are the perfect place to put this into practice. For example, if we forget to pack towels and the kids get wet, they can dry off with a sweatshirt, an extra pair of socks, or the old napkins at the bottom of my backpack. None of these are ideal, but learning to make do in less than ideal circumstances will translate into all other areas of life and be such a great help to them in the future.

Learn about people who have faced true adversity.

One of the most powerful ways my family has gained the strength to stand in the middle of misadventures is by learning about people who have walked through true adversity. It's difficult to wallow in bad attitudes about a rainy camping trip when we compare our situation with Corrie ten Boom and her time in a World War II concentration camp. Stories of triumph inspire us to be strong too.

Embrace scriptures and inspiring sayings as family mottos.

"It will make a great story later" has become a family motto that goes a long way in the midst of a difficult moment. Over the years, we've developed some others. Like when we forget half our lunch, or the snacks get wet, we say, "Well, it's not our last meal." It lightens the mood and even makes us laugh.

Bible verses like Romans 12:12 serve as good reminders when we're struggling to have cheerful hearts: "Be joyful in hope, patient in affliction, faithful in prayer." Memorizing some verses together makes them easy to recall when we need them. We also have verses or inspiring sayings posted around our home and on the T-shirts we wear so they become a part of our everyday thinking.

Chapter 7

TRY NEW THINGS

We keep moving forward, opening new doors,
and doing new things, because we're curious and
curiosity keeps leading us down new paths.
—WALT DISNEY

I was nineteen when I visited France for the first time. I was
a coleader on a missionary team, there to do repairs on a
camp for underprivileged children. Our team stayed in the
barn of a beautiful old château in the French countryside. I
helped cook for our team of twenty-five teenagers, led Bible

studies, and, on occasion, helped pour concrete or shovel dirt around the property. It was a lot of hard work. I didn't mind—that was why I came. Every little thing we experienced there was a new thrill.

I loved even the simple act of shopping at the *supermarché* for our daily bread and vegetables. It was there I tried a chocolate croissant for the very first time. We didn't have such fancy pastries in the small town I grew up in. Until the day I walked into that French supermarket and smelled the heavenly aroma, I had no idea such magic existed that put chocolate inside of croissants. And when I tasted it, well, my life was forever changed.

One moment, though, stands out in my memory. It was our first afternoon off from our work project. We traveled into the nearby village, a tiny spot where the streets were narrow and lined with houses that had lace curtains and window boxes full of bright red geraniums. I was in charge of a handful of teens who all wanted to shop for candy and souvenirs.

"Before we do any of that," I told them, "we're going to find a sidewalk café, and we're ordering espressos. We're in France, for heaven's sake!" I was determined to experience the France I had read of and dreamed of for so many years. And to show those thirteen- and fourteen-year-olds that there was more to experience in foreign lands than candy bars and Coca-Cola. I wanted them to experience something new, something a little outside their comfort zone even, because I knew it would change them forever.

We found a little café with those wicker chairs you see all over France. The owner came out to talk to us and find out why all these American teens were in her village. We explained. She smiled and left to get our drinks. When she returned, she carried our coffees and bottled sodas and one big, beautiful French tart. It was covered in apples caramelized in butter and sugar. "Welcome to France!" she said, grinning happily at us. She set the tart on our table with a flourish, and I'm fairly certain my eyes filled with tears of gratitude, joy, and wonder.

In that moment, France was forever etched on my heart. It was such a sweet and simple act of kindness, but one I'll never forget. Whenever I think of that afternoon, I am so grateful. Perhaps it explains why I am intent on introducing new experiences for my children. I know the beautiful, lasting memories they bring.

Many years later I reconnected with one of the young teens from that trip. We were both adults now, married and with a handful of children each. As we reminisced about that summer we spent in a small village in France, I asked him if he remembered that special moment at the café. "Yes!" he exclaimed. "We all wanted to get candy and soda, but you urged us to try something new. I got an espresso with you. It felt so grown up and continental. I'm glad you pushed us."

Sometimes the new experience is big, like traveling to another country. But isn't it funny how, while we were in another country, the temptation was to revert back to the comfortable and familiar? However, because we didn't, we grew a bit more. While my motivation to have a new experience that time was mostly selfish, I'm still glad for the imprint it made on those kids. We made a memory that day. We connected with one another, with that sweet café owner, even with the country of France, all because we were willing to do something different.

INSTANT BONDS

From the time I was a little girl, I have always loved the thrill of "new." Whether it was trying new food, visiting new places, meeting new people, or even having new experiences in the books I read, new things filled my soul with happiness and delight. Sometimes the anticipation—the planning for and dreaming of the new thing—was just as much fun as the experience itself. For me, new things meant excitement. Adventure was surely ahead.

Of course, new things also meant the unknown, and that sometimes felt scary. New things stretch us. They can push us outside our comfort zones, and that doesn't always feel good. But I liked the idea of conquering fears or challenges, and I especially liked the feelings of accomplishment and pride that came as a result.

More than anything, though, when I think of new experiences, I think about the way they've connected me to the people I was in them with. Sometimes I was with people I'd known for my whole life, like my dad and mom. Or with my husband or kids, who I also know very well, obviously. But other times the connection has happened with complete strangers. Time and again I've been adventuring with a group of strangers, exploring new places and seeing new things, and, within days, we make a connection. We become partners in the adventure and then friends.

Experiencing new things together creates an instant bond. There is no denying the power of shared experiences to build community and connection. We create memories together and then share them forever. It's such an incredibly easy yet incredibly powerful way to make heart connections that will never, ever disappear.

> Experiencing new things together creates an instant bond.

One year, when the kids were all nine and under, we were studying stars and space for science. Each term we'd study a new science topic with our homeschool group and try to incorporate a field trip or two on the topic, culminating with a day of presentations by the kids. We always did our best to plan field trips and read books that would make the learning come alive, but one mom in our group, Marina, particularly excelled at this. She was always pushing us to go on a "next-level" field trip and trying to show us we were capable of far more than we thought we could do.

She sent out an email reading something like this: "Friends! I have an amazing opportunity for us to take our study of stars and space to the next level! My friend is a commander at Vandenberg Air Force Base and is leading a launch of a satellite there in a few weeks. He has invited our group to come to the base and see the launch. Isn't that amazing?"

I was fully on board for the adventure. I knew, however, there had to be some stipulations. For starters, the base was about four hours away, so we'd have to account for that.

Marina's email went on. "Of course, there are some logistics to figure out. The launch is scheduled for 6:00 a.m., and we'll need to be at the gate of the base for check-in at least an hour before that. And then there is a drive to the spot on the base where we'll watch the launch. So we really need to be at the base by 4:30 a.m. at the latest."

I knew it! Her big, new ideas often pushed us outside our comfort zones, and honestly, outside what seemed to make sense for a group of moms with lots of young kids. But at the same time, I knew this was an experience not to be missed. We'd be awfully tired the next day. But it would be fully worth it.

We decided that we'd drive up the day before and spend the night in a hotel together and then caravan to the base. We'd have to wake our kids at 4:00 a.m. to get to the base on time. That did not sound fun to anyone. But adventure sometimes calls us to do things we wouldn't normally choose to do. "It will be worth it," we kept telling ourselves. "It will be worth it."

Due to the upcoming launch, most hotels in the area were booked. And since we needed a block of rooms for our whole group, it was even harder to find a place to stay. We finally settled on a hotel that fit our budget, but not necessarily our standards of cleanliness. The kids didn't seem to mind that the enclosed pool was so heavily chlorinated we could hardly breathe from the fumes. They didn't notice that the carpet was worn and stained or that their moms were slightly freaking out about dirty bathrooms. To them it was all magic. This was their first time taking a road trip and staying in a hotel with all their friends—and seeing a rocket launch too! It was the most amazing combination of new experiences, all rolled into one.

I didn't sleep much at all that night. Partly because I was worried I'd oversleep and mess up the caravan to the base for the whole group. And partly because I was worried about bedbugs. The rational part of my brain said there weren't any bedbugs. But the middle-of-the-night, haven't-slept-a-wink, I'm-on-a-road-trip-with-my-four-small-children-by-myself part of my brain said there were.

At three o'clock in the morning I gave up, got up, showered, and packed our bags. I set out warm clothes for the kids, blankets, and an on-the-go breakfast to eat in the car. It was kind of a zoo when we all made it into the lobby. Tired kids and tired but excited moms. In between the yawns and commiserating about no sleep—"I was up all night too!"—we were laughing. "Only Marina could make us do this!"

Inviting someone new into our circle can feel scary. Especially if she introduces us to new ideas, new ways of doing things, or new adventures. It may be uncomfortable or even nerve-wracking to give "new" a shot, but it's so important for us to be open to the change. Because change is what brings about growth.

We all want our kids to grow, to be exposed to new ideas, meet new people, and have new experiences. We expect that as a normal and natural part of childhood. However, as parents, we sometimes forget that this is important for us too. That's understandable. Because while we all like the idea of new things in theory, actually putting those new things into practice can feel daunting, difficult, and, yes, even a little bit frightening. That's totally okay! That challenging space is where the growth is going to happen. We'll grow as individuals, and we'll grow together in our relationships with one another. So say yes to the people, the books, and the experiences that push you into the new. Remember, they are actually helping you grow.

INVITING YOUR KIDS TO OVERCOME

Outside the air was crisp and cold. Forty degrees! Practically freezing for us Californians. We filled every minivan to capacity, trying to take fewer vehicles onto the base. I drove off with my own four kids and two more, one of whom was a two-year-old crying loudly for her mama in another car. The road was dark, and we were out in the countryside. We all shouted with excitement when a coyote crossed the road in front of us. I played happy music to wake us all up and get little Audrey to stop crying.

We were about halfway to the air force base when I realized the tags on my car were expired. "Oh, dear Lord," I prayed, "please don't let that keep us from getting on the base. And please don't let them look too closely at my driver's license." I had a sneaking suspicion it was expired too. Geez.

"Guys, we have to pray!" I called over the music and the still-crying two-year-old, now joined by my two-year-old.

"Why, Mommy?" they asked.

"Because I just remembered that I didn't put a sticker on the car that it is supposed to have, and I don't know if they care about things like that at the base. But we have to pray that they don't and that we can get in."

I turned down the music and prayed aloud over the crying. I was pretty sure there would be no problems with my expired tags and getting on the base. But just like my tired brain worried about the bedbugs the night before, a part of me was worried right now. Letting the kids into the problem didn't mean I was scaring them. It meant I was showing them that we don't have to handle any problem on our own.

New adventures take us into the unknown. Sometimes that means simple misadventures, or it might mean real struggle. Whatever it is, as a parent, that's your time to invite your kids in to help problem-solve, push through, or pray. Or probably all three. This kind of honesty creates more connection. There is the opportunity to come together in the hard spots, and when you find your way out of them, to

> New adventures take us into the unknown. . . . Invite your kids in to help problem-solve, push through, or pray.

celebrate that overcoming together. It makes the memory all the more special.

As we pulled up to the gate, one minivan in a line of others, the kids all prayed quietly that the soldier would let us in. He did. With hardly a glance at my license, but a look at his list of vehicles to let in, he simply said, "Enjoy the launch, ma'am." As soon as we pulled forward, we all erupted in cheers. "We made it! God answered our prayers! We're going to see the rocket launch!" Our little unexpected hiccup had just made the trip even better.

We followed an official vehicle through the base until we came to an empty grass field. We piled out of the cars, wrapped in colorful Mexican blankets and with binoculars around our necks. Far in the distance we could see the rocket, shiny white and lit up by the brightest spotlights. It was a beautiful sight. The soldiers with us passed out special patches to the kids and showed them a model of the rocket being launched. We all marched around, holding babies, drinking coffee, and trying to keep warm. We moms knew there was always a possibility that the launch could be canceled, even at the last minute. So we held our breaths and prayed for no complications. We weren't sure our kids' overly excited and overly tired hearts could bear a cancelled launch.

But soon the soldiers had radio contact, and they told us all to get ready. We stood together, looking toward the rocket, and counted down, some kids covering their ears and others jumping up and down with excitement. Even though the rocket was miles away, we heard the roar of the engines and watched it lift into the sky. Shouts rose into the air along with it. It was like nothing we'd ever experienced before. None of us will ever forget it.

Nothing feels quite so adventurous as doing something new or visiting a new place. When I first considered regular adventuring with my kids, doing new things and seeing new places were two of my top priorities. That's because I knew these new experiences would pull us together.

If you're wondering how you can incorporate new adventures into your family's life, here are some ideas to get you started!

For those who want to grow their tried-and-true adventures into something new:

- Take a hike in a wilderness park instead of a nature center.
- Take a rock-climbing class rather than climbing the jungle gym at the playground.
- If you've never been camping, rent or borrow a tent and camp out in the backyard.
- Instead of driving into the city for a day of adventure, take public transportation and expand your adventure.
- Take a familiar hike with a foraging expert and see everything with new eyes.
- Rather than going to a children's museum, take your children to a "grown-up" art museum.

- Take everyone to lunch. But instead of going to your favorite spot, go to a food hall where you can adventure with new food. Have everyone try one new thing of their choice.
- Find a national monument nearby that you never knew about and visit it.
- Try swimming/tubing/kayaking in a creek, river, ocean, or lake—whatever body of water is new to you.
- Take your kids to a symphony, ballet, or play. Even if they can't sit through the whole thing, give them a taste of it.

For those who want to have an adventure that is all new:

- Find out when the next big meteor shower will be and drive to a dark sky space to watch it happen.
- Plan a camping trip and let the kids be in charge of making the menu, shopping for the food, and cooking it. Maybe help them out by being in charge of cleanup.
- Take a longer hike than you have ever done before.
- Learn to do something you've never done: fishing, horseback riding, surfing, painting with watercolors, pottery throwing, or ballroom dancing.
- Make a new food that feels so challenging to you, you aren't sure you can actually do it.
- Sign up and train for a 5K, a triathlon sprint, a cycling race, a mud run, or some other kind of physical activity that will push you beyond where you are now.
- Visit a completely new city or town and spend the day getting to know it. You don't have to go far at all, just someplace utterly new to you.

Chapter 8

REVISIT FAVORITES

Traditions are the inventions of people who mean to
routinely put love and comfort and meaning into their
lives and in the lives of those they live with.

—ELIZABETH BERG

I inspected my eight-year-old self in the mirror: pink Bermuda shorts, a pale green and white striped seersucker button-up shirt, pink tennies, and a too-big-for-me San Diego Padres baseball cap to keep the sun off my face. We were going to the fair. And that required more than the scruffy play clothes I ran around in all summer. These were my nice play clothes. Not so nice as a dress, because one couldn't ride the swings or fly down the bumpy slide in a dress. But nice enough to show the importance of the day ahead. A whole day with Mommy and Daddy, fair rides, fair food, and time spent wandering through the animal barns and exhibit halls when Mommy and Daddy tired of the noise of the fun zone. It was one of the most anticipated days of summer, and one we looked forward to all year long.

Walking through the gates, the sights, sounds, and smells of the fair assaulted our senses. Funnel cakes, grilled corn, deep-fried everything, and smoke from twenty-five different food stalls, all selling the "World's Best BBQ," filled our nostrils and turned our minds instantly to the one treat we'd get that day. Oh, it was so hard to decide! Every year I wanted to try the giant dill pickle or an order of hot, crispy Australian potato chips. But every year, I ended up with the same chocolate-dipped ice cream bar from the Olde Tyme Ice Cream shop. It was my favorite. And it was tradition.

My little brother wanted to run to the rides, but our parents wanted to linger in the home and garden exhibits. They admired prizewinning dahlias and intricately shaped bonsai trees. We admired the giant backyard spas, dipped our hands longingly in their warm, bubbling water, and asked like we did every year, "Didn't they used to let kids swim in these sometimes? If they brought their suits with them?"

And, like every year, the answer was the same: "One time they let your big sister and brother play in them because

Dad had a booth for the whole fair. It was a hot day, and they felt bad for Jay and Kristen sitting in the booth all day."

Ben and I sighed together. "I sure wish we could go in them."

Funny how magical those big jacuzzies seemed to us each year. Our admiration for them and longing for a dip never waned.

The rest of the day was long, hot, sweaty, and so much fun. We screamed with delight from atop the swings. We all felt a little bit sick from the Tilt-A-Whirl. When we were older, we even braved rides like the Gravitron. That was a ride shaped like a flying saucer that spun so fast you were basically held against the wall for the whole ride. Pitch-black darkness and ridiculously loud music made the experience all the more disorienting.

The animal barns made us think fondly of Wilbur and Fern from *Charlotte's Web*. We loved seeing prize rabbits, chickens, and guinea pigs. And, even more, the big farm animals raised by kids who had yards large enough for a pig, a lamb, or a cow. Sometimes we'd have art in the youth exhibits, and there were few greater thrills than seeing a ribbon next to our watercolor painting or pencil drawing. All these things we did year after year, yet that fact didn't diminish our joy in them.

Sometimes we fear that repeating the same adventure will become boring to our kids. We think they'll roll their eyes at us and say something like, "Not this *again*!" And perhaps they will say that if we repeat the same adventure too often. Most of us would tire of that. But when done correctly, repeated adventures bring benefits we might not expect.

There was something so dear and wonderful about our yearly adventure to the fair. The repeated adventure became a tradition. The tradition became a collection of memories. And the memories drew us together.

Each time I walk back through those fair gates as a grown woman, still with my dad but also with my four children, I experience the power of tradition. The same smells, sights, and sounds fill my head, and I'm transported back to my childhood. And then to the years of fair trips I've made with my own kids. They're part of the adventure now. I watch them try to decide between a dill pickle, onion rings, or Dippin' Dots. The same decisions I had to make, yet just different enough to make the story their own. My kids also love hearing the "swimming in the spa" story as we walk through the home and garden exhibits. It is so deeply moving to relive my childhood memories while simultaneously making new ones with my kids. I can't help but think that one day we might be doing this with their kids. All of us bound together by years of adventuring and making these shared memories—connecting us to our past and to one another.

A MEASURE OF GROWTH

Returning to adventure, especially year after year, is a wonderful way to measure growth. It's not forced in any way. We're not setting out to prove to our kids that they can more easily do the thing that used to be so much harder for them. It is just a natural byproduct of repetition. So many times we'll finish a hike we've done before and one of my kids will say, "Wow! That hike was so easy. Remember when it used to be so hard?"

For the past twelve years our family has vacationed in the same spot on the California Central Coast. The entire trip has become rich in repeated adventures. So many favorite adventures, in fact, that we can't make them all happen in one week. We have to pick our most favorite from the favorites list and then make sure we do the ones we missed the year before.

One adventure that always makes the list is kayaking in Morro Bay. It's an incredibly beautiful and unique spot on the coast. A miles-long sandbar stretches down from beachside cliffs, cutting off the pounding ocean waves and creating the peaceful bay. The little town sits on the hill above the bay, with fragrant eucalyptus trees scattered amid funky beach cottages. It's one of the prettiest spots I know. That is, until you get out on the water. Then it gets even better.

We tried kayaking here for the first time when the kids were all too young to be in their own kayaks. We weren't sure how two adults could take four kids kayaking, but the lovely man who owned the boat rental shop showed us how the smallest kids could sit between the seats of a two-person kayak. He instructed us to give the sea lions a wide berth, cautioned not to get too close to the sea otters, and explained how to use the tide to paddle back more easily. "Remember," he said, smiling at us, "however far you paddle out, you'll have to paddle that far back." Knowing I'd be paddling the kayak mostly myself, I had a hard time imagining we'd make it all the way to the end of the bay. I was just thrilled we'd finally all be making it out onto the water together. It was going to be an epic adventure.

I don't recall all the details from that first paddle around Morro Bay. I know I wiped tears of joy from my face when we pulled up to watch an otter float on her back, an abalone shell balanced on her chest. We could hear the rhythmic thump, thump, thump as she hit the shell repeatedly with one fin. When it cracked open, she managed to get the tender abalone meat out, and then she flicked the shell right off her chest. There were many squeals of delight at watching something with our own eyes that heretofore we had only read about in books. I remember some of the kids were nervous of the barking sea lions, and others urged us to go just a little bit closer. And I recall that tiring paddle back to the boathouse. My shoulders burned by the end.

Each time we return to the bay, it's the same, but also a little bit different. We greet the man at the boathouse, who by now has become an old friend. We see the same sea lions, and the rafts of otters still thrill us. We inhale the same scents of salty air and eucalyptus. We always hunt for sand dollars and sea hares in the shallow water by the sandbar. But from one year to the next, the paddling becomes easier, because as the kids grow, they're more able to help propel us across the water. One year our friend at the boathouse looked at our older boys and said, "I think they're ready for their own kayak now, don't you?" And just like that, our familiar adventure became new. The adventure hadn't changed, but we had.

This shift in how we experience this adventure doesn't make it any less enjoyable. In many ways it makes it more enjoyable! Of course, it's easier to paddle only one kid around the bay instead of two. But much more significantly, the kids can see their own growth. As we paddle out, the big boys delight in their newfound freedom. And the younger ones are making plans for the day that they get their own kayak too. When we pull up on the sandbar and spread out for a picnic, we all begin to reminisce.

> The adventure hadn't changed, but we had.

"Remember when we got caught in that windstorm and could hardly paddle back to the boathouse?"

"Remember when that seal popped up right next to our boat?"

"Remember when we almost crashed into that sailboat?"

"Remember?"

"Remember?"

"Remember?"

These "remember when" conversations are connection at its best! They are a beautiful measurement of each child's growth. Best of all, it's a growth we have all experienced together, year after year, as we've revisited this beloved spot.

SURPRISES WHILE REVISITING FAVORITES

Our Adventure Club excels at revisiting favorite adventures. Part of that comes from necessity, of course. After eleven years of adventuring together, many adventures need to be repeated. But each year when we make plans and put our adventures on the calendar, we consider the years before. We know the kids' favorite adventures. We know the best time of year for all the different adventures. We anticipate heat waves, winter rains, seasonal tours, and springtime wildflower blooms. And we plan accordingly. All our knowledge, experience, and planning, though, still can't rule out the element of surprise. And that is just so much fun!

One of our favorite destinations became a favorite because of the surprises we keep encountering there. The first time we visited, there actually wasn't much to see. It was just a dried-up pond, dusty and filled with big chunks of dried-up mud that the younger boys in the group had great fun throwing at each other. The rest of the kids were unimpressed. But we moms knew that dried-up pond was actually something called a vernal pool. After a winter of heavy rains, the pool would be filled with water and also teeming with plant, insect, and animal life. When the next winter blessed us with lots of rain, we scheduled the vernal pool as one of our adventures, hoping it would be better for us than the last time we visited.

Sure enough, when we reached the top of the hill and looked down on what had been a boring, dried-up pond the year before, we saw it was full of water. "There wasn't water here last time!" someone called out excitedly. The kids all dashed down the hill. Within minutes they were filling the air with wild screams from every direction.

"Frogs!"

"There are frogs! Millions and millions of frogs!"

"It's amazing! They're coming out of the ground!"

"They're tiny!"

"They're swimming!"

"This is so cool!"

We mamas ran down the hill to join them, and, indeed, there were millions, or at least thousands, of tiny frogs. It really was amazing. We felt like we had walked straight into one of the biblical plagues from Exodus. Except it wasn't a punishment. It was one of the best surprises ever. Tiny frogs climbed out of tiny holes in the mud and dirt and made their way toward the water. They hopped over our feet, into our hands, out of our hands, and plopped into the muddy pond where they swam away.

The next year, almost every kid and mom in our Adventure Club had the vernal pool listed as a favorite adventure and one we wanted to repeat. Excitement about seeing the frogs again was high. But, oh, the sadness we all felt when we crested the hill, looked down, and saw no pond. Either there wasn't enough rain to fill it, or it had already dried up.

The following year, when we again planned a return to the vernal pool, some kids complained. "Not again! There were no frogs last time. It's so boring when there is no water." Sometimes revisiting adventures comes with initial opposition because we are holding onto memories that aren't the best. But we decided to push forward and hope we'd be rewarded with another surprise. Some of the kids were skeptical. Some were optimistic. Others were hopeful. Everyone perked up when we saw water in the pond. But, from a distance, we didn't see any sign of movement. We didn't see any frogs.

> Repeated adventures become tradition. Traditions become memories. And memories draw us together.

"Maybe they're so tiny you can't see them until we're closer," said one of the more hopeful kiddos. But it was definitely a more sedate crew that marched down the hill toward the pond. No frogs. How could we have missed them again?

Then someone yelled, "Tadpoles!"

A new surprise from this place we thought we knew so well! The pond was teeming with tadpoles. Some areas were absolutely black with their shiny, slithering bodies. You could pick up tadpoles by the handful. We'd never seen anything like it.

There are wonderful benefits to returning to the same adventure multiple times. When we return to the same hiking trail, cultural event, or family tradition year after year, we create a longing for that shared experience. It's something to look forward to. That is how we want our kids to feel about these adventures they take with us. Those memories will hold a special place in their hearts for the rest of their lives. I don't go on adventures with my kids just for the connections they create now. I also adventure with them to create connections that, I hope, will last a lifetime. I'm in this for the long haul. And I'm not afraid to revisit our favorite adventures year after year. Because I know that repeated adventures become tradition. Traditions become memories. And memories draw us together.

If you're looking for adventures that are perfect for repeating with your family, here are some ideas to get you started!

Seasonal:

- **Winter:** Plan an excursion that can only happen in winter—snowshoeing, cross-country skiing, ice fishing, snow tubing, or visiting an ice garden. Bring along a thermos of hot cocoa or hot soup, and have a picnic in the snow or in the back of the car bundled up in blankets if it's too cold.

- **Spring:** Keep an eye out for the peak wildflower bloom in your area. Research local trails, nature centers, and wilderness parks to find out where the most wildflowers grow, and then make a day of visiting one of those places. You can take a guided hike with a wildflower expert or just bring your own field guides and identify the wildflowers on your own. This adventure can happen every spring. The wildflower bloom will come at a slightly different time each year, to different spots, and with an abundance of different kinds of flowers, but that will be the surprise!

- **Summer:** Kick off summer or bring summer to a close with an annual camping trip. Whether you return to the same spot or try a new destination, the campout itself will be the familiar adventure. Make sure you add in activities that are family favorites—a s'more-making competition, singing silly songs around the campfire, hiking to a swimming hole or creek, or earning a Junior Ranger badge with the campground rangers.

- **Fall:** Make the most of fall by enjoying traditional activities like visiting an apple farm and making pressed cider. Or take a nature walk through the woods or your neighborhood and collect brightly colored fall foliage. You can press the leaves between the pages of a book to dry, or dip them in hot beeswax to preserve them longer. Make pumpkin bread and share it with friends or neighbors.

Holidays:

- Plan a New Year's Day adventure—a hike in the snow, a walk on the beach, a picnic at a nature center—and while there, talk about all your favorite adventures from the year before.

- Host a Valentine's party for your kids' friends. Have them trade valentines with one another and make valentines for people in need of cheer—folks at an eldercare home, a sick neighbor, or kids at the children's hospital. I promise, it will be an adventure to have all those kids at your home making valentines!

- Go on an early morning Fourth of July hike, paddle, or swim. Get outside together before you spend the day eating all that good BBQ.

- Make Thanksgiving weekend about being together instead of shopping. Plan a camping trip or a weekend at a cabin. In time, the trip will come to be just as important as the Thanksgiving dinner.

- For Christmas, bake a big batch of treats to share with neighbors and friends all over your town. My family makes giant batches of cinnamon rolls, hundreds of them, and because it is such a big project, it definitely feels like an adventure. Then we package them up, don Santa hats, and drive all over town delivering them. It's something we look forward to every single year, and it brings joy to us and the people we bring fresh-from-the-oven cinnamon rolls to.

Chapter 9

DO HARD THINGS

You never really understand a person until you
consider things from his point of view . . . until you
climb into his skin and walk around in it.
—HARPER LEE

It was time. Our Adventure Club had been talking about it
for a few years now but hadn't worked up the courage to
actually do it. We didn't want to stall any longer. We decided
to be brave and do this hard thing. We would take our kids
camping by ourselves.

As moms of kids all under ten, some of them toddlers or babies, camping without our husbands as backup felt like a big undertaking. All of us had camped before, but never had we carried the weight of the responsibility solely on our shoulders. We had always had our men there to pitch the tent, build the fire, and, more than anything, provide a second pair of hands and eyes to help with and keep track of all those little people. We knew it would be harder to camp without the extra help. But we wanted to show our sons and daughters that their moms could do this, so that one day, when they wanted to go camping on their own, they wouldn't have to wait for backup to be available to go with them. Far more important, though, was letting them see that doing hard things was not only possible but very worth the effort.

I pulled up to the campsite, already feeling victorious because I'd survived the two-and-a-half-hour drive through Los Angeles traffic, passing snacks back to the kids and getting the audiobook to the right spot, all without a copilot. The kids and I got to work right away, unloading the car and chasing two-year-old Davy back to the campsite when he ventured too far. There was so much stuff. I'm a notorious overpacker, and since this was my first solo camping trip, I had outdone myself. We laid things out on the picnic table as I tried to decide what to do first.

"Probably the tent, guys," I told the kids. "Let's get the tent up."

Just then, one of the kids yelled, "Mommy! There's a squirrel in our food! Now there's a squirrel in our car!"

I turned to look, and sure enough there was a squirrel *inside* one of the brown paper grocery bags holding things like hot dog buns, marshmallows, and hot cocoa mix. He popped his head out of the bag and jumped out, scurrying around the back of the car before he jumped back in the bag with all the food.

"Ahhhhh!" I screamed. "What do we do?"

I'm mildly terrified of squirrels. They can get aggressive and territorial, and since they're members of the rodent family, I just know they're covered with all kinds of rodent germs. And those rodent germs were now on my food and all over my car.

"We have to get him out of there!" I yelled again, not even trying to hide my panic from the kids.

"You can do it, Mommy!" they cheered me on, from a safe distance of course.

"We need a plan, team," I told them.

No one was willing to get in the car and flush the squirrel out, so we decided on using big sticks to gently encourage him out of the car and back into nature where he belonged. The kids went scurrying off to find big sticks, and I kept yelling at the squirrel to stay out of my food and get out of my car. He didn't listen.

Eventually, with the help of the big sticks, we were able to keep him from hiding under the seats and nudge him out of the car. I was certain he'd leap from the car and right onto my head. But he just scampered off to the nearest tree where he stayed for a while, scolding us loudly. Meanwhile, we collapsed around the picnic table and laughed about how scared I was of a tiny squirrel. We also decided that next time we went camping, all the food would go in a big plastic bin with a tight-fitting lid. Lesson learned.

Next, we put up the tent together. It was not easy to remember exactly what pieces went where. Thankfully, I have a child with an engineering brain who likes to figure out how things work, and he was a big help. We assembled the tent without breaking anything, and we didn't even have any unaccounted-for pieces. By this time, other mamas were arriving and setting up their tents too. We all pitched in and helped each other through the learning curve. Looking at our campsites full of upright, sturdy tents filled us with pride and a sense of accomplishment.

Having checked tent setup off our list, it was time to get ready for dinner, which meant setting up the camp stove and building a campfire. Every time I'd been camping, I'd let my dad or my husband set up the stove and build the fire. I hadn't bothered to learn, because they were there to do these things for me. Neither thing is necessarily hard, but sometimes they can be. We've had broken camp stoves before, or fires that just wouldn't light. I wanted to be able to do these things myself—even the troubleshooting—because this offered more freedom to my kids and me for future adventures. It would be easier, and more fun, to have my husband along, of course, but since his schedule was a lot less open than mine, I wanted to be able to camp without him. This trip was the first step in accomplishing that goal.

I called on my eight-, ten-, and six-year-olds for backup, moral support, and problem-solving, and together we got the propane camp stove up and running and the campfire lit! Then, after dinner and cleanup, we all gathered around to toast marshmallows and sing campfire songs. We told stories and caught toads that were hopping through the campsite. Some of us walked out to a clearing where we could catch a full view of the stars. It was really a perfect night, and every single one of us felt so happy we had finally braved a mama-and-kids camping trip.

Of course, rarely do things ever go exactly according to plan, and some of us ended up having to brave even more when some of the kids got sick in the night. But, despite the struggles, we mamas decided we'd definitely do another moms-and-kids campout in the future. It had been hard, yes, but we had still had fun. It was worth the effort. Best of all, we realized we were stronger than we thought.

BUILDING EMPATHY FOR OUR KIDS

One of the best ways we can connect with our kids is to put ourselves in situations where we're reminded what it's like to do hard things—the struggle, the setbacks, the feelings of discomfort, and maybe even the embarrassment. Experiencing those things gives us empathy for our kids. Few things build heart-to-heart connections like empathy. If we really long to know who our kids are, there is no better way to do this than by seeing things from their point of view.

Think about it. When was the last time you did something for the first time? Or intentionally chose to do something you knew would be hard? These kinds of experiences are important. They build confidence. They help us grow. They actually breed more success. Doing new and challenging things is also really important for us as parents. Because it puts us in our kids' shoes for a while, giving us the opportunity to have empathy for their experiences.

Few things build heart-to-heart connections like empathy.

For example, think about the times you've put your kids in hard situations:

"Stand in front of that ball that's coming at you really fast, and hit it with this little stick. Don't be scared! And if it hits you, don't cry!" Or, "Go into that group where you don't know a soul and talk to people and make friends, and I'll pick you up in an hour. Don't be clingy!" Or, "Sound out these letters into words, and read them quickly, out loud, and in front of people. And you better do it before you are six. Don't mess up!"

When your child expressed fear, worry, or even frustration in response to these hard things, were you understanding and compassionate? Did you show empathy? Did you cheer and say, "You can do it!" like my kids did when I was scared of the squirrel in my minivan? Or did you just say that it was time to act like a big kid? As adults, it's easy to brush our children's feelings aside, because their troubles often are small in comparison to ours. Have you ever said something like this to your kids? (Be honest.) "You have no idea what hard is! You should try living my life for a little while." Just because our grown-up life is most likely more difficult than our kids' lives, we don't have to dismiss their feelings as they work through the struggle.

Of course, it's imperative for us to encourage our kids to try new things, to meet new people, and to learn new skills. But we must show them kindness and gentleness during the process. We need to give them grace when it's hard. We need to hug them and say, "It's okay to be scared." We need to root for them and let them know we are standing behind them or next to them, and that we always will be. If we truly want to connect with them in the process of walking through hard things, we need to understand where they are coming from. We need to do the hard thing ourselves.

So, I'm saying: go for it!

Be the new kid.

Be a beginner.

Be *not* good at something.

Struggle.

Be scared.

It will help you understand your kids.

It will help you know your kids.

It will help you connect with your kids.

Step out of your comfort zone and into your child's experiences. It will only strengthen the connections between your hearts.

ADVENTURES THAT STRETCH US

When we join our kids in adventures that stretch us, we are drawn together in powerful ways. What do these kinds of adventures look like? Well, you know the ones you kind of dread? The ones you know will be good for you both because they'll be hard? Yeah, those are the adventures we're talking about. These adventures might bring some blood, sweat, or tears along the way. But they'll also bring so much confidence, growth, and ultimately success. All while building deep connections as you walk through the adventure together.

For years I had been avoiding taking my youngest with us to see the *Nutcracker* ballet. We went every Christmas, but I always found a friend to watch Davy. I just couldn't brave sitting through a lengthy ballet with a noisy baby, a busy toddler, or an active, loud, and easily bored preschooler. It sounded like torture for both of us.

The year he turned six, though, I decided it was time to let Davy in on the fun tradition with his big brothers and sister. I didn't want to leave him out anymore. I also wanted him to grow up a little bit and experience an adventure that would be a challenge to us both. But one that would grow us too.

I knew it would take some preparation. I couldn't just dress him up in a cute outfit, whisk him off to the ballet, and hope everything would turn out okay. We began getting ready for ballet day a couple of months before the big day arrived.

We started by learning the story we'd be watching performed for us onstage. I knew it would be easier to get Davy engaged, and keep him engaged, if I could point out to him the parts of the ballet he already knew about. So we read all the picture books we could find that told the *Nutcracker* story. After a while, he fell in love with the story, and that's when I told him we were going to see it in real life. Building up anticipation is a great way to get kiddos ready to embark on an adventure that might be a challenge.

Next, I prepared Davy by playing Tchaikovsky's music for him all the time. I knew that making the music familiar would build an attachment to it, and when he heard it at the show, he wouldn't be able to help tapping his feet and being transported even further into the story.

Lastly, we talked about what to expect at the ballet. What we would do, how he would act, where we'd sit, what the ballet was like, what kind of voice to use, and even what he should do if he was bored or needed to go to the bathroom. Of course, not every kid needs this kind of preparation to go see a ballet. But mine did. I knew that planning ahead and preparing him could make this first ballet a great experience. For both of us. I didn't want either of us to spend the time frustrated or unhappy. I wanted to give Davy all the tools I could to help him succeed. I was going to push him forward, but also prepare him for the push.

Perhaps most importantly, I wanted Davy to know I believed he could do this hard thing. I wanted him to know I was on his team. One of the most powerful gifts we can give someone is the gift of belief. It is transformative. When we embark on a hard adventure with our kids, we must make sure our kids know we believe in them. This not only helps them to believe in their own ability to conquer the challenge but also knits their hearts with ours as we rise to the challenge together.

On the day of the ballet, we all had to get up early to make the drive through traffic and arrive in time for the mid-morning matinee. The kids had on "fancy" outfits, the kind Davy usually spurns with all his might. This kid who would really rather spend the day in his underwear was suited up in pants and a sweater, shoes, *and* socks, and I even combed his hair.

One of the most powerful gifts we can give someone is the gift of belief.

"This is more fancy than church," he said.

"You're right," I told him. "But we talked about it, remember? You can take your shoes and socks and sweater and pants, even, off the minute we get back into the car to drive home, okay?"

"Okay," he agreed.

When we walked into the theater, I pointed out the tall painted ceilings, the beautiful architecture, the marble floors, and the plush velvet seats. These were all the things I had told him to look for two months ago when I started prepping him for this adventure. After we found our seats we visited the bathroom and explored the lobby to get out some energy before the ballet began.

When the curtain rose, he sat up tall and loudly whispered, "Hey! It's like in the book!" He recognized the story, which was comforting and familiar and made it more fun. The music did the same thing. The familiarity of it made it so much more enjoyable. He sat through the first long stretch of the show with interest and delight on his face. I did have to coax him not to wiggle through the long, slow snowflake dance. That's when some fruit snacks hidden in my bag really came in handy. Pro tip: snacks always help. He did his best, and we made it to intermission without him having to get up early, squirm around on my lap, or have me get frustrated with him. I thought that was a big success.

By the end of the ballet, Davy was a little tired of it. He was also a little tired of sitting still and being quiet. But he hung on. And when the curtain rose, I leaned over and whispered in his ear, "Hey, buddy! You did it! You watched a whole ballet! I'm so proud of you. I knew you could do it." His face lit up, and so did my heart. We both did it.

That's when he said to me, in his loud, not-ballet voice, "Good. I get a treat now, right?"

For some, attending a ballet might not seem like much of a hard adventure. But for some kids, and their parents, it truly is. Just like for another family, going on a hike or a camping trip might feel like a difficult adventure to set out on. Remember, it's not what the adventure is but that it pushes you and your child out of your comfort zones. The challenge offers the opportunity for growth and success.

Walking through challenges together, and then overcoming them, builds confidence and heart connection.

Frederick Douglass said, "If there is no struggle, there is no progress." As parents we are often quick to point out how a struggle is good for our kids. "You'll grow," we tell them. "And you'll feel so proud, so triumphant, when you succeed." However, we don't always remember to add ourselves to the equation. We need to struggle too. And when we struggle alongside our kids, overcoming obstacles together, we not only understand each other better but also become better friends.

Not sure how to add "hard" into your adventures? Here are some ideas to get you started!

- Turn your backyard campout into a campground campout.
- Instead of a walk around the block, take a one-mile hike at a wilderness park.
- Cook dinner over a campfire instead of on the stove.
- Volunteer to regularly pick up trash at your favorite beach, park, or nature spot.
- Try snow camping this winter.
- Sign up for your first 5K, and train and then run the race with your child.
- Go on an overnight backpacking trip.

- Take a class, and learn how to do something that scares you. Here are four on my list: singing, stand-up comedy, self-defense, and ballroom dancing.
- Organize a fundraiser for a cause you care about.
- Go for a night hike to see the stars.
- See if you can still roller-skate at the roller rink.
- Instead of kayaking on a calm lake, try river rafting on some rapids.

Chapter 10

GET OUTSIDE

This sudden splash into pure wilderness—baptism in
Nature's warm heart—how utterly happy it made us!
—JOHN MUIR

My kids and I hike together nearly every single week, sometimes more than once. And while our hikes are partly about having fun, getting exercise, being with our friends, and taking our learning into the great outdoors, they are also an intentional part of my parenting. Hiking is time I spend making heart connections with my kids.

On our walks I hear a lot of, "Hey, Mom!" as each of my kids falls in step beside me to share new thoughts. Someone often slips a hand into mine. For the ones that think they are past the handholding stage, I make a point of ruffling their hair, hugging them, looking into their eyes and saying, "I love to be with you." No one is plugged into anything but the world around us and each other. It's a precious, sweet time, and one I value and protect fiercely.

The older my kids get, the more I recognize the critical importance of this ritual we have made together. My prayer when we started hiking was that when they became teenagers and young adults, they wouldn't feel awkward sharing with me in this way because we'd been doing it since they were small. Now I am right in the middle of the teen years with three of my kids, and God has answered my prayer with abundance. We talk together easily about both difficult topics and comfortable ones because we have had years of practice doing so.

When we're hiking, the conversations don't feel forced or uncomfortable. We aren't going somewhere "just to talk." We're on the trail for the sheer pleasure that hiking and being out in nature brings. The conversations and heart connections that happen as a result are simply the natural overflow of our time together.

It's such a simple solution. But for me it's already proved to be profoundly wonderful and valuable for my family.

Of course, it's important to remember that none of this just happened. This idea of "connecting through hiking" has been an intentional part of my parenting journey for a long time. When my kids were little, I made hiking a priority. I worked hard to cultivate a love for hiking in each one of them. That is a huge part of this equation. I wanted my kids to love hiking so that they'd want to keep hiking with me as they grew up. And I believed that if I started hiking with them when they were little I'd normalize it, and it would become a beloved part of our family life.

Over the years, this keeps showing itself to be true. My kids have grown as hikers, and they've learned to set their sights on bigger and better hikes. They want to climb to the top of the mountains we've only hiked partway up. They want to go on more overnight backpacking trips. They want to hike the Alps. And I want to do all those things right alongside them, talking, connecting, and building relationship with them along the way.

GETTING AWAY

There is something extra special about adventures that take place outside. Being out in nature strips away many distractions of our everyday life. Often there is no cell service. We're given a rare and needed opportunity to truly focus on each other and make those connections. It's easier to have heart-to-heart talks as we walk shoulder to shoulder on the trail. We actually have time to have a conversation, a precious commodity in our busy world. Being outside, we're inspired by the beauty around us, and natural conversation topics abound as we take in new views and experiences. Having nothing else to do but pick up shells, point out birds, admire trees, and share the thrill of finding a really awesome bug or snake builds a sense of camaraderie.

Being out in nature strips away many distractions of our everyday life.

But no matter what type of activity it is—rock climbing, mountain biking, tide pool exploring, going to the park, camping—getting outside together means doing something different from our everyday inside routine, and that makes it exciting and special. It stands out. Adventuring in God's creation makes heart connections happen in a deep and powerful way.

RESETTING HEARTS AND MINDS

Getting outside also provides a simple way to reset hearts and minds after a difficult day or week or after a rough patch, however long it has lasted. Stuck inside the house, we might feel like we can't talk to each other, focusing on all that has been going wrong. But getting out in the fresh air clears our heads and, often, mends our hearts. Adventures bring us together, even if we're feeling far apart. All we have to do is get out the door.

I saw this reset happening one day after a particularly rough week of mothering. My little Davy had pushed every button I had. William and Lilly had been bickering all day. And I had let myself see my kids as a bother far more than I had seen them as a blessing. I sighed a lot. I was exasperated. I wasn't delighting in my kids at all and really just wanted some time away from them.

So we went for a midday hike at the nature center near our house. We were all in desperate need of some sunshine and to feel the cool breeze on our cheeks. We needed the peace that time spent in God's creation brings. And I didn't mind the thought of them running ahead on the trail while I walked a little more slowly behind them. Space. I craved some space.

The trail wasn't a very exciting one. It was one we had hiked many times before. And even though we were hiking through a beautiful oak grove, we could hear the quiet, constant hum of the freeway traffic nearby. Still, the beauty of the trail spoke to us. Giant sycamore trees spread their leaves overhead. Ducks swam by on the stream. Lizards scurried across the path. I felt my weariness ease. My irritation and frustration slipped away, and I could see my children with fresh eyes.

The kids felt it too. The bickering stopped as they ran ahead on the trail, calling to each other to see this or that. They stooped to put acorns in their pockets or run back to me with a beautiful leaf. I didn't mind their shoes getting muddy when they stood on the wet creek bank. Dirty knees and hands felt like a small price to pay for the happiness we were all experiencing.

We stopped at the pond to look for the osprey we'd seen there before. William spotted it perched on a stick in the middle of the pond.

"Look, Mommy!" Excitement filled his voice. "I see one!"

The osprey was calling to another bird, and we all watched in awe as a second osprey soared right over our heads and dove into the pond. It was breathtaking. He did it again. Then another hawk appeared. A green heron sailed in. We watched the dragonflies dance on the water. William counted how many times the turtles came up for air. No one bickered, and Davy wasn't trying anyone's patience. We were just happy to be there and happy to be together. It was a quiet and beautiful half hour that was a gift from God. I didn't need space from the kids anymore. I was glad to be with them.

Adventuring outside resets our hearts and minds individually and with one another.

I whispered a "thank you, God," for my change of heart. What seemed a very ordinary walk on a very ordinary trail brought about some extraordinary moments. We had an adventure. The beautiful, amazing world around us helped us shift our focus off ourselves. Whether we're climbing the most exquisite trail in a national park or walking on an ordinary nature trail in the middle of the city, adventuring outside resets our hearts and minds individually and with one another. Our time spent in nature draws us toward God and toward each other. That's most assuredly worth the late dinners, the muddy floors, and the extra laundry that outdoor adventures inevitably bring.

The truth is, outdoor adventures do come with their own set of difficulties. There might be bugs to contend with. Or mud. Your kids might get wet when they beg to jump in the creek or the waves. Your car will probably be full of sand or dirt. You might find rocks and sticks rolling around in your dryer. You'll probably be hot and sweaty on some hikes and freezing cold and wet on others. You may not feel like cooking dinner after a long day outdoors, so you might have to be disciplined enough to put food in the Crock-Pot in the morning. Or hope everyone will be content with toast and cereal for dinner. Your bathtub could have a perpetual ring of dirt around it after the kids wash the pond gunk or playground dirt off. All of these things can feel like a big stretch for us. Are clean floors and a clean car too much to sacrifice?

While I understand the mind-set that despises the mess and, let's be honest, the extra work, this verse reminds me to treasure what is really important as I adventure with my kids: "Store up for yourselves treasures in heaven, where moths and vermin do not destroy, and where thieves do not break in and steal. For where your treasure is, there your heart will be also" (Matt. 6:20–21). I know that in twenty years I won't care about the layer of grime in my tub. But the memories we made, and the connections that grew out of every afternoon we spent out in nature, will be of so much value. They truly are the treasures of my heart.

Want to get outside with your kids? Here are some ideas to get you started!

First, gather supplies. ·

- **Get a comfortable backpack for longer outdoor adventures and a smaller one, or a waist pack, for shorter excursions.** When your kids are very young, you can carry everything yourself. But as soon as they are old enough, give them a small pack to carry on their own and get them used to carrying it on every trip.

- **Make a picnic kit so you are always ready for an outdoor meal.** Your kit should include reusable water bottles for each person, and Mom or Dad should carry an extra one. We like to carry small, lightweight, reusable bowls to eat snacks and lunch from on the trail rather than bring disposable plates and bowls. I bring a Swiss Army knife to cut fruit or cheese. I also pack a lightweight flat sheet for sitting on. It takes up far less room in my pack than a picnic blanket. We use a small cooler bag to carry all the food items that need to be kept cold. It fits inside my backpack. And I always include a large ziplock bag (the reusable kind are great for this) for any trash or food items like apple cores or orange peels.

- **Create a list of go-to snack and lunch items for outdoor adventures so that it's easy for you, or your kids, to pack food to go.** We like protein items like string cheese and salami and nuts. Granola bars or energy bars are easily portable and filling. Apples and oranges are fruits that hold up well being packed. Grapes transported in a reusable container are a refreshing treat when it's warmer. Carrot sticks and cucumbers make great snacks when paired with hummus. Peanut butter sandwiches hold up on long hikes. And I always like to pack the kids their favorite chips, crackers, popcorn, or pretzels to munch on as they hike or to enjoy with lunch. I also always pack a special sweet treat or two in my own pack or the cooler bag. This is usually helpful at the end of a long adventure when everyone needs a little boost.

- **Get field guides for the local trees, wildflowers, butterflies, and birds in your area.** Take them with you when you walk or hike and use them to learn about the nature that lives where you do.

- **Let your kids help you pack a small first aid kit for your outdoor adventures.** Include items like bandages of different sizes, antibacterial ointment, anti-itch cream, tweezers, pain reliever, moleskin for blisters, hand sanitizer, lip balm, and sunscreen.

- **Put together an emergency potty kit.** Gather a small pack of wet wipes and toilet paper, as well as some ziplock bags. Store all of these in a larger ziplock bag. If someone has to go to the bathroom while out on the trail, dig a hole about four to six inches deep for them to use, fill the hole back in when they are done, and pack out the used wipes and toilet paper in the ziplock bags.

Next, get outside!

- **Go for a nature walk.** You can walk around your neighborhood or at the park. Look for interesting leaves, rocks, sticks, or other natural bits and collect them. Identify them, sketch them, or simply display and enjoy them when you get home. This is an accessible, doable adventure no matter the age of your kids or how much time you have in a week or day.

- **Visit a body of water.** Whether it's a creek, river, pond, or the ocean, exploring the nature in and around water is different and exciting. Look for fish, insects, and other animals. Wade in. Get your feet, or your whole body, wet. One of the best ways to adventure with your kids is to actually get in nature.

- **Go rock climbing or bouldering.** This can be as adventurous or tame as you'd like it to be. If you're just starting out, research a park or wilderness area that has big rocks to climb on. These kinds of rocks don't require special equipment to scramble around on. Just help your kids learn to listen to their body and to climb with thought and caution. If you'd like more of a challenge, go rock climbing with a guide or instructor who will fit you out with all the right safety gear and teach you how to rock climb in the wild. You'll make such fun memories!

- **Try boating.** You can go kayaking or canoeing. Try out a stand-up paddleboard, or go out in a rowboat together. You can even take sailing classes together. Being on the water is peaceful and calm. It invites conversation and connection.

- **Go hiking.** Hiking is by far my favorite way to adventure outdoors with my kids. It's budget-friendly, requires very little gear, and can be as easy or as difficult as you want it to be. Best of all, hiking allows for easy conversations as you walk down a trail, shoulder to shoulder instead of face-to-face.

- **More outdoor adventures to try.** Horseback riding, mountain biking, camping, surfing, snowshoeing, backpacking, archery, cycling, trail running, campfire cooking, and cross-country skiing.

Chapter 11

INDOOR ADVENTURES

Twenty years from now you will be more disappointed by the
things you didn't do than by the ones you did do. So throw
off the bowlines. Sail away from the safe harbor. Catch the
trade winds in your sails. Explore. Dream. Discover.
—H. JACKSON BROWN JR.

You ready for tomorrow?" I asked my son James, not even
trying to hide the excitement in my voice.

"Not really," he replied, not even trying to hide the indif-
ference in his voice.

I laughed at him, gave him a tight hug, and said, "You might be surprised, James, and discover you really like it."

He shrugged, and I grinned. I wasn't going to let his lack of excitement dampen my own. Starting a new thing is hard. Especially when it's something your mom wants you to do and something you're not sure you'll like. I understood where he was coming from, so I didn't press him to match my excitement and joy about our upcoming adventure.

My alarm went off at six o'clock the next morning, and I reluctantly rolled out of bed. As excited as I was for James to join me in my morning workout, I still hated getting up early and getting ready for the gym. I expected I'd have to wake James and maybe even push him a bit to get going. He surprised me, though, by getting up on his own and being dressed and ready—still not excited, but willing. That was a gift from my fifteen-year-old boy.

I understood his hesitation and his nervousness. After all, it wasn't that long ago that I was walking into my first boot camp class feeling so nervous I worried I might throw up or have diarrhea in the middle of a jumping jack. But I also knew that, if he could persevere through the first class, the first week, and even the first month, he would discover new parts of himself. It would be worth the push. I was excited to see the transformation take place.

He survived that first workout. It was a hard one. For me even. More so for him. Trying to follow along, feeling the awkward uncomfortableness that happens when you haven't been running and all of a sudden you have to. He was red-faced, tired, sweaty, and hungry when we were done. And not terribly talkative on the way home.

I suggested we go again in a couple days.

"I think twice in the first week sounds good, do you?"

He shrugged and said, "I guess."

I just smiled at him and teased, "I'll take that as an enthusiastic yes!"

Guess what? Three classes in he was joking with me as we worked out side by side. When our trainer shouted encouragement to us to finish our last few sprints on the treadmill—"No one made you come here today! But you came anyway! Finish this run!"—James leaned over to me and said between heaving breaths, "That's not true. My mom made me come today."

I laughed so hard I had to hold on to the handles of my treadmill to not go flying off the back. And that quickly became our favorite joke. "My mom made me do it."

Transformation was happening in James for sure. I didn't have to wake him up for workouts. He was proud of each new milestone reached. He wanted to talk to me about the workouts after we finished them, comparing what was hardest for each of us and complaining about sore muscles the next day. He loved getting his stats and seeing how he was running farther and faster with each workout. There was a newfound confidence about him. There was a literal pep in his step each time we walked in the door after a finished workout. Witnessing these changes was such a blessing to my mama heart.

The part that was even more exciting, though, was the transformation happening in our relationship. James and I have always been close. We enjoy each other's company. There is no awkwardness or distance. But even when there is no distance, there is still room to grow closer. There is room to create connection. And that was what these early morning workouts at the gym were doing for us.

ADVENTURING AS PARTNERS

Depending on where you live, there are times of the year when indoor adventures are a must. And sometimes, like James and I working out together at the gym, the adventure takes place indoors no matter what the weather. Some parents might worry that indoor adventures are a poor substitute for adventures in the grand outdoors. But that just isn't true. Indoor adventures provide a unique opportunity to experience different things with our kids. This is our chance to get to know our children better and in new ways.

We might see what kinds of things our children are interested in learning more about or trying for the first time. Or this might be the time we invite our kids into our world, including them in the activities that excite us. Doing it together becomes the adventure. Learning a new skill together puts parent and child on the same level and creates such a fun and unique dynamic in the relationship. Lots of laughter happens and camaraderie grows. That brings such ease to the work of building heart connections.

It was certainly the case with James and me. We weren't just a mom and a son who were working out together. We were friends. On that very first day at the gym, I decided to step out of the role of parent and into the role of partner. It changed everything. I wasn't there to nag James, count how many squats he did, or even look like I was dissecting his performance. I was there as his workout buddy. To grumble with him about an extra hard routine. To laugh with him when our coaches pushed us and we wanted to hide from them. To tell him how strong he was. To encourage him to keep going when he felt like giving up. To speak praise. When I became that person for him, he thrived, and so did our relationship.

> Learning a new skill together puts parent and child on the same level and creates such a fun and unique dynamic in the relationship.

Honestly, I wasn't expecting this as an outcome of exercising with my son. I wasn't even looking at this activity we were going to do together as an adventure. I just saw it as something James needed to do, and the easiest way to help him do it was by having him do it with me. I saw myself as his accountability, which made it feel more like a punishment or a chore to him. When I realized it didn't have to be that way, working out together became our adventure.

So often we expect our kids to be on board with our new ideas. We expect them to jump for joy even though the thing we're presenting doesn't sound very exciting for them. It's okay to give them time to warm up to the idea. It's even okay to let them not like it for a while until you prove to them that the adventure is going to be worth it. We have to be willing to prove that to them. We have to partner with them, adventure alongside them, learn with them, and grow with them.

There are many ways to pursue these indoor adventure-as-partners moments. If you're nervous to take a class or try an activity because it is all new to you, please try it anyway! Being on level ground with your child brings a new kind of closeness and creates solidarity as you work together through the learning curve.

A friend of mine took a pottery class with her daughter. Every Tuesday night the two of them sat at potter's wheels near each other and threw bowls and vases and jewelry holders. They had a blast connecting over wet clay and creating visual reminders of their time spent together in the form of beautiful glazed pottery.

If the adventure is an activity your child is already interested in, then all the better! They'll have the opportunity to bring you into their world. They get to be the expert and teach you!

TRY, TRY AGAIN

I know for some of us, the prospect of taking our kids to a class or event that is more structured or formal, such as visiting the art museum, can fill our hearts with utter dread. "Take my wild things to a place where they must be quiet or pay attention for an extended period of time? Or somewhere they can't run and touch or must be extra careful so as not to hurt themselves or others? Surely you must be joking."

I promise you, I'm not. You can do these things. You can take your kids to the art museum. Or to pottery class. Or to pastry baking or indoor rock climbing. Before they're twenty. And you can actually have fun there. All of you. It will be an adventure!

For me, going to the art museum with my kids was a day I had long dreamed of. The boys had their sketchbooks in hand, pencils sharpened, with extras stashed safely in their backpacks. They were ready to observe art and then make some of their own. We were at the Norton Simon Museum in Pasadena, California, to see a special exhibit of Degas's horse sculptures. James and William had been taking a sculpting class, and their teacher suggested they visit this exhibit. He assured them that the opportunity to see Degas's sculptures up close, to study them and sketch them, was incredible. So we went.

Walking calmly through the museum with my teenage sons, I felt tears filling my eyes. I almost couldn't believe we were here together, them willing and excited, me free of anxiety and nerves. Trips to the museum in the past had left me sweaty, stressed, and overwhelmed. I wasn't the mom I wanted to be there, and the kids didn't have the art museum experience I wanted them to have. All the rules about not touching, not running, being quiet, not climbing, just didn't jive with my busy little people. The thought of them somehow destroying a priceless work of art gave me heart palpitations. But I wanted them to love art museums. I wanted them to have favorite artists and be excited to see their works in real life and not just flat and lifeless on the pages of a book. I didn't visit an art museum until I was in college, and I felt like I had missed out on so much.

So I tried. My oldest is a natural observer and artist. He actually loved visiting the art museum. Rules didn't feel oppressive to him, but safe. My other kids, though, didn't see it that way. I remember one day when I decided to brave the art museum on my own with all four kiddos. My youngest was one and a half; I could keep him safely strapped in the stroller. The others would stay near me and listen to me, I reasoned. What I didn't count on was the way my toddler would twist his whole body with a relentless desire to get out of the stroller. Or the way I'd feel so uncomfortable under the stares of other museum goers and the guards when my baby boy raised his voice in loud protest to being stuck in that stroller. I didn't count on the boredom my second son would demonstrate with his whole body as he flopped dramatically onto a bench in yet another room of "boooor-rrrinnggg paintings." I didn't count on the way they'd all be overwhelmed so quickly by seeing so much art.

There were lots of whispered promises of "we'll have treats later if you just be quieter!" Or even whispered threats in that crazy, fake-calm mommy voice we all muster at one time or another. James couldn't really enjoy the museum because his siblings quickly tired of sitting and looking at paintings while he could have looked at them much longer. By the time we left, all I could think of was that maybe they wouldn't go back until college.

My mistake, of course, was that I didn't have a plan. I thought that by simply exposing my kids to the museum often, they'd grow to love it. That might have worked for one or two of my kids. But the others, the ones who felt rules were an oppression, needed something more. They needed small, manageable doses of the art museum. They needed to interact with the museum and the art there in a way that was fun and inviting and not just a long list of "don'ts." I changed my strategy.

I realized I needed to put work in on the front end and make visiting the museum a treat for my kids, not a chore. After all, if I hoped to visit art museums with my adult children one day, sipping cappuccinos together and looking for our favorite Van Gogh, I needed to help that happen *now*. Like all relationships, their relationship with the art museum was going to take some work, time, and investment.

We'd visit the museum again. But some other things would have to happen before we did.

First, I began to teach my kids about museum etiquette. Instead of just going over the long list of don'ts, I explained the whys behind the don'ts. That led us to begin learning about art history and art restoration. We learned about famous paintings that had been lost, found, and restored and were now hanging in museums to be enjoyed by many.

We talked about how to act when we saw nude paintings or statues. We didn't have to laugh or point. We didn't have to feel embarrassed or ashamed. That opened a conversation about nudes that were beautiful and a celebration of the human body, one of God's most amazing pieces of creativity. But we also talked about the nudes that made us feel uncomfortable or yucky and were not a celebration of the human body, and what to do when we saw those. Look away, move to another part of the museum, and tell Mommy, "I don't like that one."

Our conversation then turned to Michelangelo, one of the greatest sculptors of one of the most famous nudes, *David*. I showed them pictures of *David*, and we read some books about Michelangelo. I began to stockpile children's books about art and artists and art history and read them as part of our regular rotation. All of these things opened up my kids' minds and hearts to the art that filled museums. They became interested in paintings, sculptures, and artistic movements because they heard the stories behind these things. Stories are such an incredible way to create connection, not only with one another but also to art.

When we finally returned to the museum, I put my plan into action: make it manageable, make it meaningful, and make it fun. And it worked! I designed a scavenger hunt for the kids to find a small number of works they recognized or pieces by artists they knew. This helped them avoid the art coma that can come from taking in so many pieces of art that they all blend together. It made the museum experience manageable.

Because they were looking for pieces and artists they knew, the time spent at the museum was meaningful. And because they got to walk around the museum with clipboards and a check list, it was fun! We ended the day with my kids saying, "Thanks for taking us here, Mommy. We really love this museum."

My formerly self-proclaimed museum-hating son said, "Yeah, I thought art museums were the dumbest. But this was actually fun."

Make it manageable, make it meaningful, and make it fun.

James, my little art lover, asked, "Can we come back sometime and sit on those benches in the galleries and just look at lots of art?"

Even the toddler had a good time and didn't touch a single priceless piece of art.

I called it a win and totally worth the blood, sweat, and tears it took to get there.

Sometimes it's weather that encourages us to adventure indoors, and sometimes it's a desire to learn a new skill or hobby. But whatever the reason, we can be sure that indoor adventures create bonds between our kids' hearts and ours. Adventures are all about stepping into new things, and indoor adventures provide just the space for that.

I love indoor adventures because they allow us to step into each other's lives in new ways. We can pursue shared interests, discover new passions together, experience the satisfaction of serving others, or simply enjoy making something beautiful together. All of these things help us get to know our kids at a deeper level, as the unique individuals they are. Even if it takes years to get to the place where we can experience these things together, the benefits will last for many years to come.

If you're looking for indoor adventures to try, here are some ideas to get you started!

Classes to take/things to learn together:

- Calligraphy writing
- Watercolor painting
- CPR and lifesaving
- Public speaking
- Jewelry making
- Silk screen printing
- Ukulele or banjo playing
- Knitting or crocheting
- Wood carving
- Spanish or Chinese or some other foreign language
- Sculpting
- Cartooning
- Sewing
- Cake decorating
- Sushi rolling
- Self-defense training
- Hula dancing

Other indoor activities or events that can turn into mini adventures: · · · · · ·

- Volunteer together at a local senior center and play cards or board games with seniors.
- Commit to serve regularly at a local rescue mission or shelter.
- Work at a local animal shelter.
- Join the choir at church together.
- Go to see a play or musical.
- Take a trip to an aquarium.
- Watch a ballet.
- Go to an indoor climbing gym.
- Visit a science center.
- Go to a children's museum.
- Stroll through a conservatory.
- Try out parkour.
- Visit an OCR gym.
- See an indoor sporting event.
- Visit an art museum.

Chapter 12

ADVENTURING WITH BOOKS

That is what a book does. It introduces us to people
and places we wouldn't ordinarily know. A good book is
a magic gateway into a wider world of wonder, beauty,
delight, and adventure. Books are experiences that make
us grow, that add something to our inner stature.
—GLADYS HUNT

ost people don't think of books and adventure belong-
ing in the same sentence. If someone were to describe
a bookworm and an adventurer, I am certain two very

different pictures would emerge. Some people find reading books to be a tame activity at best and a boring one at worst. As an avid reader and lifelong lover of books myself, I'd counter and say they're just reading the wrong books. I have actually had some of my greatest adventures in the pages of books. I have traveled the world, met incredible people, and had incredible experiences as I have read books. Books contain adventures.

Books make adventure accessible.

This is especially wonderful if you are a person who is unable to, for whatever reason, go on many adventures. Perhaps your family doesn't have the means to travel abroad. Well, if you read a book that takes place in India, guess what? You've had an adventure there. Perhaps you or your child has physical limitations that make activities like hiking, snowshoeing, or rock climbing impossible. When you read a book about a character who does those things, you've tasted a bit of that adventure yourself. Books make adventure accessible.

MAKING THE MOST WITH WHAT YOU HAVE

Growing up, I went on many adventures through books. My mom was not what you'd call outdoorsy or a lover of adventure. She loved and appreciated nature but liked to experience it in a comfortable way. Like bird watching from the living room with a cup of tea. Or, if she was feeling very adventurous, working in the garden. She did not enjoy outdoor adventures unless my dad was along because she was worried about things like getting attacked by a mountain lion, a random bad guy hiding in the woods, or snakes. But even if my dad was with us, outdoor adventures often made her nervous. They stressed her out.

And she didn't like dirt—on her, on us, or in the house.

To complicate matters further, she had back injuries that made physical activity very difficult and often painful for her. So there were a lot of reasons I can't recall her ever taking us on a hike or camping trip. But even if all those things weren't standing in the way, there were other issues that made exploring nature difficult.

Our family was often strapped for money. My dad worked very hard, but he was a self-employed artist and then a pastor of a very small church. Not a lot of extra money in either of those careers. And my mom didn't work outside the home. The extra money needed for long drives to see natural wonders often wasn't available. And, much of the time, my dad took our only car to work, so even if we had the gas money, we didn't have a car to drive.

This was hard for me sometimes, because I loved the outdoors and adventures. I longed for them with all my heart. It would be easy to look back on those days of my unfulfilled longing for backpacking trips, tide pool explorations, and hikes in the woods and see a lack. It would be easy to think that my parents didn't attend to the desires of my heart. But that wouldn't be the truth. Because God stepped in where there was lack, and he filled in with his abundance. God gave me adventures through books.

My mom is a great reader. She loved books and passed that love onto every one of her four children. That's a legacy right there. My parents could have lamented the fact that they didn't have enough money to take us on backpacking trips or to visit the Grand Canyon. My mom could have been depressed that her body wasn't physically able to take us hiking or that she wasn't emotionally up to it. But as far as I could tell, she didn't dwell on the limitations. She made the most with what she had and trusted God to fill in the gaps. And one of the ways he did that was through books.

I vividly recall sitting on our big brown couch with my mom as she read aloud to us from books that were absolutely full of adventure. We read about Laura Ingalls Wilder and her family who traveled west across the country in a covered wagon, dealing with blizzards, grasshopper invasions, wolves, and malaria. We read *Where the Red Fern Grows* and cried together as Billy and his beloved coonhounds won the silver cup in the coon hunting contest. We trembled with Anne Shirley as she waited to find out if Green Gables would be her forever home. The books and characters my mom introduced me to loved adventure as much as I did. They lived it. Even more, they were written by authors who knew about adventures and made it an important element in their books. Those books filled a void in my adventure-hungry soul. They fanned the flame and fed it at the same time.

Reading these sorts of books introduced me to adventures I probably would never know otherwise. When I read *The Yearling*, I watched the dance of the whooping cranes, even though I had never visited a swamp in my life. I adventured alongside Jody and his pet fawn, Flag. After reading *The Secret Garden*, I could feel the wild, cold loneliness of the English moors every winter and their warmth and life in the spring. I traveled the world through books, and it absolutely filled that adventure-shaped hole in my heart.

These books and many others are an incredibly important part of my childhood. So much so that, when I was getting married, my mom gave me *The Little House Cookbook* as a gift at my bridal shower. That cookbook represented a collection of memories and all the time we had spent together reading the Little House books. The characters' adventures in the books had somehow become our adventures too. And the experience of reading them together bonded us forever.

You see, the magic of reading was about more than just going on adventures through books. Reading books was special because I got to go on adventures *with my mom*. As I said before, Mom wasn't much of an adventurer. She left that to my dad. But when we read together, the adventures became ours, and we connected between those pages. Her physical inability or our lack of funds didn't matter when we were reading. The books took us on the adventure.

For some families, like my own growing up, adventures have to look different. Whether it's due to physical limitations, financial limitations, or something else, these families need to find a way to adventure from home. Books offer an incredible way to do this. When you're reading together, you are sharing the same journey, caring about the same characters, laughing over the same jokes, or mourning the same heartache. Reading together builds relationships.

When you start reading aloud to your child, where does your child sit? In your lap, right? Then, as your kids grow, they snuggle up next to you on the couch or in bed. So right from the start you are creating all kinds of beautiful, warm, comforting connections as you read books together. You are telling them, "This is where we connect. This is where I spend time with you. This is where we laugh together and where I don't look at my phone. This is where we learn new things and go on adventures. This is our place." From the time our kids are very young, reading brings closeness and connectedness.

Books help us make the world bigger for our kids.

Once you've established reading books together as a special way to connect, a world of adventuring together awaits. Jacqueline Kennedy Onassis said, "There are many little ways to enlarge your child's world. Love of books is the best of all." And it's so true. You can introduce your children to new places, new people, new ideas, and new experiences through books. There is no way I can take my kids all the places in the world I want to. Or experience all the things with them I'd like to. But through books, we can do an awful lot of adventuring together. Books help us make the world bigger for our kids.

BEGINNING A FAMILY JOURNEY
OF READING TOGETHER

If your family is not accustomed to reading together, the idea of starting this up can seem daunting. But you can help your kids grow a love of books and begin your family's journey of reading together through just a few simple steps.

Start by making your home into a book-rich environment. No matter how little or big your kids are, fill their rooms and your whole house up with books! Board books, picture books, big beautiful books with illustrations, library books, reference books, art books, young adult novels, classics, and comic books. All. The. Books. If there are books all around them, your kids will be drawn to them.

Next, make reading time regular and make it special. Read a book together in your bed or theirs when they first wake up. Read before bedtime. Have a special time in the morning when you read about Jesus and sing a song and pray together. Have afternoon tea and book time. Read together every single day, throughout the day, and make sure you are fully present when you read. Put your phone down! We can't expect our kids to want to connect with us if we're sending the message that we aren't fully invested in connecting with them.

Next, be sure you read the best books! Spend time looking for good picture books with beautiful illustrations and great storytelling. Look for old books at the used bookstore. Ask other moms what their favorite books are for their kiddos. Don't just get those books with the kids' favorite cartoon character on the front cover. Invest in the books that are going to require a little more time to read aloud and a little more effort for your kids to understand. It is so worth it, because those are the books that often have the best adventures.

Also, visit the library often. I know the library can be hard when your kids are small. It's like the art museum. I totally get it. The fussy baby, the crazy toddler who is climbing the bookshelves, the overdue fees—I've done it all. But if you make a regular habit out of going to the library with your kids, even if you only stay for ten minutes to start with, at some point they are going to fall in love with the library. They are going to ask to visit again. They are going to go in, grab a book, sit down, and read. Then they'll bring a stack home and read some more. Build a love for the home of books.

After you come home from the library, or even on the days you don't go, you have to give your kids time for reading. Whether they're reading with you, reading on their own, or listening to an audiobook, the time to read is a valuable gift. I spent so much of my childhood reading books. My mom allowed me plenty of time for this. I even got in trouble for reading too much. But I consider it one of the greatest gifts my parents gave to me. So, don't be afraid to let your child be in less classes and activities. Provide unstructured time and a stack of good reading material, and let your kids be lost in the world of books. It will pay off in the end.

Another way to help your kids grow as readers is to read them books above their reading level. Starting at about age three, you can really begin to challenge them. Read them longer picture books. Read them the real Beatrix Potter collection and not the simplified versions. Read them chapter books, even if the stories are a little above their heads. If you are constantly giving them more, they'll rise to the occasion. The language and syntax and storytelling will be a challenge for them, but you'll be amazed at how much they get out of reading more difficult books.

One of the best ways to expose your kids to books that are above their reading level is through audiobooks. In our family we are huge fans of audiobooks. I love the way listening to them brings us all together. I'll often find my kids spending an entire afternoon listening to a book together, sometimes while drawing, building with LEGO blocks, or just lying on the couch or floor and soaking up the story. Other times we'll listen to a book while we drive. In those cases, the kids actually look forward to longer car rides, because we'll have more time with our book. Even chores like folding laundry can be done together with more enjoyment when we're listening to a book as we fold a mountain of towels.

These precious times together are the making of relationship: we laugh, sometimes cry, and we talk. We have beautiful conversations about whatever story we are listening to. We all relate to the book in different ways, but we experience it together and each share what it brings up in us. We talk in the language of the books we've read. I often hear my kids say things like: "You know that part in *The Hobbit* . . ." or, "It's like in *Caddie Woodlawn* when . . ." The books we read together create cherished memories just as family vacations and adventures do. The books we've read together are some of our favorite adventures.

Reading and listening to books together has become one of the most powerful tools for connecting our family. Remember, you don't have to go on fancy vacations or grand adventures to create memories with your family. Making memories and creating connections can be as simple as popping a bowl of popcorn and settling down with a fabulous audiobook. You'll laugh together, wonder together, and if you're like my family, cry together. Best of all, listening to a book takes some time, so you'll get to revisit that togetherness again and again until the book is done. And the memory of the adventure you all had as you journeyed through the pages of the book will stay in your hearts forever.

No matter the age of your children, you can adventure together through books. Here are some of our favorites to get you started!

Books for younger readers (but very much enjoyed by older readers too):

- The Little House series by Laura Ingalls Wilder—be sure to read all nine books.

- *The Railway Children* by E. Nesbit
- The Chronicles of Narnia by C. S. Lewis—be sure to read all seven books in the series.
- *Mr. Popper's Penguins* by Florence and Richard Atwater
- Mrs. Piggle-Wiggle by Betty MacDonald—be sure to read all five books in this series.
- *Rascal* by Sterling North
- *Danny, the Champion of the World* by Roald Dahl
- *The Tale of Despereaux* by Kate DiCamillo
- The Green Ember series by S. D. Smith—be sure to read all four books.
- My Side of the Mountain trilogy by Jean Craighead George—be sure to read all three books.

Books for older readers (younger readers can enjoy alongside their parents due to more advanced reading level or more mature themes):

- *The Yearling* by Marjorie Kinnan Rawlings
- The Anne of Green Gables series by Lucy Maud Montgomery—read all eight books to journey with Anne as she goes from a preteen girl to married mother of seven.
- *Where the Red Fern Grows* by Wilson Rawls
- The Time Quintet by Madeleine L'Engle—be sure to read all five books.
- *Sweep: The Story of a Girl and Her Monster* by Jonathan Auxier
- The Wingfeather Saga by Andrew Peterson—be sure to read all four books in this series.

- *Little Women* by Louisa May Alcott
- The Mysterious Benedict Society by Trenton Lee Stewart—be sure to read all five books in this series.
- *Island of the Blue Dolphins* by Scott O'Dell
- The Lord of the Rings trilogy by J. R. R. Tolkien—older kids might enjoy this series a few years after reading *The Hobbit*.

CONCLUSION

Call to Action

Wherever you are, be all there!
—JIM ELLIOT

*T*he bitter cold wind whipped around us as we stepped from the warm bus. I pulled my coat tighter around my body and pulled my scarf up higher on my neck. Our guide quickly moved across the parking lot and toward a small stand of olive trees. *Maybe he's hoping they'll provide some shelter from the wind*, I thought as I followed him. My nose ran and my eyes watered. It was so very different than what this Southern California native was used to. And even though it was February, it was still quite different than what

I expected from Greece. I guess it wasn't always warm and sunny and filled with vacationers in crisp white linen and sun hats. Greece was downright freezing.

This was certainly different than the last big adventure Dad and I had gone on together more than twenty years ago. Back then we were in southern India, doing all we could to stay cool in the sweltering heat. Back then I was a teenager, just beginning to find my place in the world. Now we were shivering together in the cold, atop the most famous hill in Athens. Now I was a mother of four, always busy and distracted.

I hadn't spent more than half a day alone with my dad in probably fifteen years. Since my first child was born, my dad had sweetly begun taking my kids for an afternoon or day to give me a break, but we hadn't had much time alone with each other. I still couldn't believe we were adventuring together again. Just like old times. Yet so much more precious now, because I had the benefit of many years to remind me that time like this with my dad was not so easy to come by. And it was certainly not to be taken for granted. Time together was a gift. That we still wanted to adventure together: another gift. All those years he'd spent creating connections with me as a little girl, a tween, and a teen were still bearing fruit. And the evidence was us standing there in Athens on our first visit to Europe together. It only took us forty-two years to make it happen.

I struggled to hear our guide over the roar of the wind as we trudged up the hill toward the Acropolis. Halfway up, we stopped in front of a small, rocky outcrop. "This is Mars Hill," our guide shouted. "Paul stood right there and debated the Athenians about the existence of God." We all looked at the rock with wonder. We were going to walk in the footsteps of one of the Bible's most beloved figures. We would tread the very ground where the apostle Paul had trod. Amazing.

What with the wild wind and rain earlier in the day, the rocks of Mars Hill were slippery. Our guide suggested using the stairs with sturdy handrails built into the side of the rock. But if we really wanted to walk in Paul's footsteps, we could climb up the rough and rugged steps carved directly into the rock two thousand years ago. Dad and I looked at each other and grinned. There was no need to say a word. The spirit of adventure that beat in both our hearts said one thing: "Go!" So we did.

Not bothering to worry about slipping or getting blown off the top of Mars Hill, we climbed those steps together. Atop the rock, we were fully exposed to wind so strong it was difficult to stand upright. But we laughingly took pictures of one another with the Parthenon in the background, standing in the same pose, arms stretched wide to the joy and possibility of that moment and of all the moments to come. Our arms and hearts were open to adventure and open to one another. It was a moment I'll never, ever forget. And I'll be forever grateful I said yes to adventuring with him.

Months before, Dad had called me and I could hear the excitement in his voice as he said, "I have something to ask you."

"Okay," I replied, expecting him to ask me to help teach vacation Bible school or commit to reading through the Bible with him.

"I'm going to Greece and Turkey for twelve days," he said, "and I want you to come with me."

My heart leaped in my chest. Oh, how I wanted to say yes. I wanted to jump right in and be fully committed in that moment. But I hesitated. Yes, I, the girl who is always ready to adventure, wasn't sure. There were so many things to consider. I'd never been so far from my children. I'd never left them for so long. What if Aaron couldn't take the time off to stay home with them? Could we afford the cost of such a trip? Would traveling with my dad again go smoothly now that I was a grown woman, used to caring for herself and making her own decisions? Would we drive each other crazy? All these thoughts filled my head as I listened to my dad talk about every detail of the upcoming trip. "Let me ask Aaron," I told him as we got ready to hang up. "Let's see if we can actually make this happen."

I told Aaron when he got home from work, and without any hesitation at all, he said, "I think you should go." Wow. Okay, babe. But Aaron's rationale was strong. "You never know when you'll have the opportunity to take a trip like this with your dad again. It's a chance for you to take the trip of a lifetime with your dad. You don't often get opportunities like this. Just do it. We'll make it work."

And we did. Oh, it wasn't easy. Saying yes to adventure often isn't easy. It takes work and sacrifice and preparation and often saying no to other things. Sometimes it takes other people coming alongside you to help. It means being vulnerable and inviting people into the adventure with you. It means being vulnerable during the adventure and letting others see how you respond when things become difficult or problems arise. Saying yes to adventure means being willing to risk that the experience will be a big flop. But it also means believing that the journey will be incredibly wonderful.

In the weeks leading up to our trip, my heart was torn in two. One of my dearest friends was dying of cancer. And as the day of my departure approached, she grew worse. I didn't want to go. I didn't want to leave her in what would most likely be our last days together. There came a day when I knew I had to ask her, "Do you want me to stay?" We sat together in her room, me wearing a mask and her without one to make it easier for her to talk.

"I want you to go on this trip with your dad," she told me in her belovedly bossy way before I could even bring up the subject. "There is no way you're missing this. And if I pass while you're there, I still want you to have fun. I want you to enjoy every minute of your time there. Just because I'm dying doesn't mean you should stop living."

I smiled at her through my tears. "Yes, Jen," I said. "I'll go. And I'll be taking this trip with you in my heart."

She laughed with her glorious, loud laugh, and our talk turned to other things. I knew I had to go.

Still, when the day came to say goodbye, it was so hard. I drove to her house the night before, praying with all my heart that it wouldn't be the last time I saw her. I didn't want to leave. I didn't want to leave her. I kissed her cheek and promised, "I'll see you soon."

It was every bit as hard as I expected and so much harder. I packed into the night. And in the morning, I felt sick to my stomach at the thought of saying goodbye to my own family. I travel fairly often now but had never experienced these kinds of emotions. Maybe because I was going so far. Maybe because I'd be gone for so long. Maybe because of Jen. Maybe because of all of it.

Our Uber pulled up in front of the house. I hugged my kids tight, kissed my man on the lips, and didn't try to hold back the tears as I waved madly to all of them out the back window. Within two minutes of being in the car, my dad had already informed our friendly driver that this was his first ever ride in an Uber, that we were headed out on an adventure to Greece and Turkey, and that the last time we'd traveled together I was eighteen and we were going to India. Then he asked our driver if he went to church. I settled back into my seat with a smile as I wiped the tears away. This was going to be fun. This was going to be an adventure! And despite all that I was leaving behind, I decided I was going to soak up every minute of the time God had given me with my dad. It was a full-circle moment, and a gift.

As parents, one of our greatest fears is our children drifting away from us. When they're little the fear isn't as real, because we are still the center of their universe. But with each year, they become more independent and we think we're losing them. This isn't really the truth. Their becoming independent doesn't mean they don't need us. It just means they don't need us to wipe their bottom, pick out their clothes, or drive them to school. But they still need our presence, our friendship, our encouragement, and our love. They need to know we support them and that we believe in them. They need to know we won't pull back from them, even if they push us away. They need to know we'll hang on!

Adventuring together provides a space and a place for this to happen. The time together doesn't have to be forced or awkward. When we are willing to put in the work, the connections will begin to happen naturally. Especially when we spend time together doing some of the activities I've shared in this book. Know that this will take time and sacrifice and effort on our part. We can't expect our kids to put down their phones and clear their schedules for us if we won't do the same for them. We can't expect connection with our kids to happen overnight if we've been neglecting it for years. You are on this journey together for the rest of your life, so keep moving forward together, making memories, and having adventures and trust that the heart connections are being made slowly but surely.

> Be all there with your kids, and you'll reap the rewards for the rest of your life.

It will be work.

There may be whining when the hills are steep and the sun is hot. Sometimes there will be coaxing and cajoling and bribing. There may be repeated reminders of, "We're just looking—we're not touching" and, "We don't climb things in museums!" Potty breaks will always happen in awkward places. There might be heavy babies and supplies to carry on our back. Breastfeeding and diaper changing might happen on the trail. And every adventure will probably involve sweat or tears—often a bit of both.

But. If we persevere, there will be magic.

There will be wonder.
There will be joy.
They will discover the caves.
They will find beauty in the mundane.
They'll learn how to knit or sew.
They will catch the grasshoppers and the ladybugs.
They will roll down grassy hills.
They will stop to pick the wildflowers.
They'll make jam and bake cakes.
They'll serve meals to the elderly and the hungry.
They will climb tall trees.
They will wade in the stream.
They'll thrill at the sounds of the symphony and the sights of the ballet.
They will sink in the quicksand.
They won't be afraid to get all kinds of dirty or wet.
They will jump in and *live life*.
And we will get to be right there with them!

This is what I'm wishing for you today. And in all the days ahead. I'm wishing that you go out and meet your kids on the hiking trail, at the art class, in the tent in the backyard, and in the pages of the book you are reading together. I pray that you will adventure with them, and that, by doing so, you'll build connections that will last a lifetime. Moms and dads, be all there with your kids, and you'll reap the rewards for the rest of your life. Adventure awaits!

HOW TO CREATE AN
ADVENTURE CLUB

*O*ur Adventure Club began eleven years ago, with the simple idea that we wanted our kids to spend a large chunk of time outside together every week. We moms knew we'd be more successful at making this happen regularly if we were part of a group. The accountability and time with friends would help motivate us. Our kids were all ages five and under, so, at first, we just met at local parks and let them play. After only a few weeks of this, we realized we wanted something more than just sliding down the slide and playing in the sand pile. So, we cast a vison for the group. We discussed all the things we'd like to do together, and the idea for going on adventures together was born.

Over the years, our group has discovered we enjoy all different kinds of adventures, but being outside and hiking are our favorite. The majority of our adventures include those activities. We also love reading books together, so book clubs have become a part of our Adventure Club. We've watched our kids grow up together, and besides becoming more and more adventurous themselves, they've become the very best of friends. Us moms have too. We dream that one day we'll be taking our grandkids on the same kind of adventures we take our kids on now. We are in this for the long haul.

If you're interested in starting your own Adventure Club, here are some details to get you going:

First, cast your vision for your Adventure Club by answering these questions:

- What are your goals for the club?
- Are you looking to build relationships?
- Are you looking to have kids grow in an area of knowledge like nature study, outdoor skills, or art history?
- What kind of adventures will you go on? Outdoor? Indoor? A mix of both?
- Do you simply want to experience adventures together, or do you want specific learning or accomplishments to take place while out adventuring?

Then, figure out the dynamics of the Adventure Club by answering these questions:

- What ages of children will attend your club?
- Will your club be just for moms and their kids, parents and kids, or just all the kids and you?

- What is the maximum number of families you want in your group?
- What kind of commitment do you expect from the involved families?
- What kind of behavior do you expect from the children attending?

Lastly, figure out the logistics of the Adventure Club by answering these questions:

- How often will you meet? Once a week, once a month, or once a quarter? (Remember, regular meetings are essential for building relationships.)
- Will you be eating a meal together? Will it be picnic style, potluck style, or at a restaurant?
- Will you have a set cost for being part of the club or let each family cover the cost of adventures as they come?
- Will one person plan all the adventures, or will you plan them as a group?
- Who will be in charge of emailing information and reminders?

Once you have answered some or all of these questions on your own, go ahead and share your idea with others who you think would be a good fit for your club. Ideally, you'd host a kind of introduction meeting where you'd share your vision and even the dynamics and logistics of how the club would work.

Then, when you have some families ready to join you, you can begin to put the ideas into action for your very own Adventure Club!

HOW TO HIKE WITH KIDS

As you know by now, I started hiking with my kids when they were all quite young, ages five to newborn. Through the years, we've all grown in our ability to hike longer distances and to take on more challenging trails. We've also grown to love hiking and now consider it to be one of our favorite family activities. Hiking is one of my favorite ways to connect with my kids.

If you're considering getting started with hiking, here are a few tips we've picked up and made a part of our hiking routine. Try putting some of these into practice with your own family!

TAKE YOUR TIME

This is critical for success, especially when your kids are young. Toss your expectations for a quick hike out the window, and everyone will enjoy the hike so much more.

PULL OFF THE TRAIL TO
EXPLORE OCCASIONALLY

Whether you're looking at an interesting bug, searching for wildflowers, or climbing a tree, it's okay to get distracted. Remember, it is about the journey, not the destination.

EAT SNACKS WHILE YOU HIKE

Sometimes we all need a little boost of energy or a distraction while climbing an especially tough hill.

COLLECT NATURE TREASURES AS YOU HIKE

Unless collecting is prohibited, we pick wildflowers and find seashells, acorns, lizard skins, and beautiful rocks. The kids bring small bags or containers to keep their treasures in and take home as mementos from the hike.

HIKE WITH FRIENDS

Hiking with friends makes hiking even more fun. When we want to do a longer or harder hike, we often meet up with friends to make conquering that challenging hike easier.

LET THE BIGGER KIDS HIKE AHEAD

As they've become more accomplished hikers, we've given the older kids freedom on the trail. At first, they had to stop when they couldn't see us. Then they could hike out of sight but had to call back using our special call. When we mamas didn't call back, that meant they had to stop. Now that they are teens, they can hike beyond our call, as long as they know the trail and stay together. It's safe independence, and it makes everyone happy.

GIVE YOUR KIDS TIME TO BECOME HIKERS

If you are new to hiking with your kids, be sure to give them some grace as they grow into hikers. Don't expect they'll magically become hikers on the first hike. Remember you are in this for the long haul, so don't make it intense in the beginning. Start slow and let your kids fall in love with hiking so they'll be hiking with you until you are the one needing them to slow down.

HOW TO ENJOY
A MUSEUM TRIP
WITH KIDS

Most of us are familiar with children's museums and even feel like we can take our kids to one without becoming a hot, sweaty, stressed-out mess. But regular museums are a different story altogether. Many parents would like to take their children to a museum that isn't just for children but are overwhelmed at the thought of it. They wonder, *How will I keep our kids quiet? How will I keep them from running around or from touching priceless works of art? Can kids and parents actually enjoy a museum trip together?*

I didn't grow up going to any museums that weren't geared specifically for children. Especially not art museums. But I was determined to write a different story for my own kids. I knew it was going to take some work to teach them how to act at a museum and, even more important, how to actually enjoy their time there. But, through thoughtful preparation, realistic expectations, and practice, I've seen them embrace museum trips and even look forward to them.

Here are some tips so you can have an enjoyable adventure to the museum with your kids too!

BEFORE YOU VISIT

Teach your kids how to act in a museum. Tell them they'll use inside voices and walk instead of run, and teach them how to look for the line on the floor that runs around the room in front of the art. Then explain that they'll stand behind the line when they are looking at the art.

Check out books from the library about museums and what it is like to visit one.

Go to the museum's website and see their most well-known pieces. Choose a few pieces you think your child will like best and write down the names of the pieces and the artists who created them.

Next, do some research. Print up pictures of the paintings or sculptures you identified or find them in books. Show them to your children and talk about the art. Ask them what they like, what they don't, and what the art makes them think or wonder about. Get to know the pieces of art like they are friends.

Get to know the artists too. Let your children learn their names and their stories.

When you are ready to visit, make a surprise scavenger hunt for the kids. The scavenger hunt can be as simple as small photos of the art pieces they have been studying. And then maybe a piece or two by the same artist that they haven't seen yet. When they find the piece, they'll put a check mark by the picture.

Print up the scavenger hunts and put them on clipboards.

All of this work done ahead of time will make your visit to the museum so much more familiar and therefore comfortable and exciting.

WHEN YOU'RE THERE

Time your visit so your kids aren't hungry or tired. Midmorning is a wonderful time. If possible, go on a weekday to avoid weekend crowds.

When you arrive at the museum, tell your kids they are going to look for some special pieces of art. Then give the kids their clipboards with the scavenger hunts and a pencil.

Use the museum map to find the pieces of art you are looking for.

You can enjoy other art along the way, but don't spend much time stopping to look at all the art. Museum fatigue is real and will only make the museum experience less meaningful for everyone, especially the kids.

Be sure you finish your time at the museum before the kids tire out. Don't worry if you aren't done with the scavenger hunt. You can always come back another time to finish it.

End your day with a stop at the children's room of the museum for hands-on playtime, or visit the café for a little treat. Finishing on a high note is the perfect way to ensure both you and your kids will want to visit the museum again!

HOW TO START
A BOOK CLUB

When I was a little girl, I longed to be part of a book club. I tried to start one when I was about eleven years old, but it didn't last longer than a few meetings. My friends didn't really want to talk about the books, and some of them didn't even read them. I tried to boss everyone around, and, really, I don't think it was much fun for any of us.

I've learned a few things since then about having a successful book club. My kids and I have been a part of one for about eight years now. It's a kids' book club, but the moms play a big role in making it a success. And our book club is, indeed, a success. Every part of it, from the books we read together to the book celebrations we have when we finish a book, is very much anticipated. I can't say enough good things about being a part of a book club. It will take your adventures with books to the next level.

If you or your kids are interested in doing a book club, here are some steps to help you get started.

CAST YOUR VISION FOR THE BOOK CLUB.

Do you want a club that is just about enjoying books together? Would you like to facilitate discussions about the book? Do you want to do activities related to the book?

DETERMINE A READING SCHEDULE.

Our club reads four books a year, one per season. It is a good way to keep from being overwhelmed by too many books but also to keep engaged with what we're reading.

DECIDE WHAT TYPES OF BOOKS YOU'LL READ.

Our book club reads mostly classic kid lit. But if a family wants to read a book that isn't on the classics list, they just have to check with everyone to see if it is okay.

DECIDE WHO WILL CHOOSE THE BOOKS.

Will you have complete book-choosing authority? In our club, we take turns choosing the book. Each family gets a turn. This allows for a lot of variety and for us to be exposed to books and genres we might not otherwise choose.

PICK AN AGE GROUP.

You can have a group that is just the ages of your kids or a mixed group. Our group is a mixture of ages. The little kids rise to the occasion on the most challenging books. If the discussion goes too long, they leave the discussion area and go play somewhere quietly.

Plan your meetings or celebrations.

After finishing a book, you want the club to interact with the book and each other in some way. That's the fun of a book club! Our club has a book celebration for every book. They are a lot of fun and the perfect way to close out a book when we finish reading it.

Here are some of the things we make a part of our book celebrations:

- **Costumes:** It is a lot of fun to dress up like characters from the book or from the time period in which the book takes place.
- **Food:** While reading the book, we keep a list of the foods mentioned. Then, each family signs up to bring some of the food from the list.
- **Discussion:** Whichever family picked the book leads the book discussion. They plan discussion questions ahead of time and choose questions for all the age levels that will be part of the discussion.
- **Games, activities, or crafts:** Sometimes the book lends itself to more than just a discussion and feast. With those books, we've added things like leatherworking, a treasure hunt, a musical parade, trying exotic foods, and so much more.

ACKNOWLEDGMENTS

Writing this book is the realization of my childhood dreams. I still can't believe it's real! I've learned so much through this whole process of book writing. One of the most important being that one does not write a book alone. And I owe a debt of gratitude to the many people who have helped me get to this moment.

Aaron, thank you for teaching yourself to cook while I wrote this book. The kids would have had far too many frozen pizzas if it hadn't been for your newly acquired skills in the kitchen. Is there anything you can't do?

Thank you for spurring me on when I wanted to give up, assuring me I could finish when I doubted myself, and understanding me when I was afraid. Thank you for letting me chase my dreams. You are my best friend.

James, William, Lilly, and Davy, thank you for adventuring with me. Without you and your stories, this book wouldn't be here. Thank you for your graciousness while I wrote. Thank you for picking up my slack around the house, for hugging me when I was overwhelmed, and for being excited with me over every little thing along the way. I love you all so very much.

Mom, thank you for giving me my love of books. It's that love of books that made me want to write one of my own. And thank you for taking me on so many adventures through the pages of the books we read together. I will never forget them.

Dad, you passed on your thirst for adventure to me. First by telling us stories at bedtime and then by making our life a grand adventure. Whether it was a trip to the lumberyard or a trip to India—you made it magic. I'll never forget our adventures; they are so dear to me.

Adventure Club mamas and kiddos, I am so grateful for our years spent together, hiking, exploring, learning, and adventuring! I love each one of you. These stories belong to all of us. Danielle and Jen, two of the OG adventure mamas—I know you're enjoying the greatest adventure yet. I miss you both so much.

To Mom and Dad Eskridge, Mom and Dad Wujek, Jana, Karen, and April—thank you for all your help with the kids whenever I had a big deadline to meet or just needed room to write. You are a part of this, and I could not have done it without you.

To my friend, Ainsley Arment, thank you for believing in me and giving me a place to use and grow my voice. To my friend Sarah Mackenzie, who told me I had to write a book, whether I was ready or not, and then helped me get started.

To my friend Anjuli Paschall, who walked a few steps ahead of me in this book writing journey and helped me as she did.

To my incredible agent, Teresa, we both know this book would not be here without you. You have been my guide, my mentor, my cheerleader, my advocate, and my friend from day one. Grateful for you doesn't begin to cover it.

To my editor extraordinaire, Jessica, thank you for pushing me to make my book better. I recall the panic attacks and the late nights, and the exact moment when I saw my book growing better before my very eyes. I owe you so much!

To the rest of the dream team at Thomas Nelson, thank you for making my book a reality. And thank you for putting up with my questions and missteps as I figured out how this whole thing works. Your guidance has been invaluable.

Lastly, I want to thank all of you, my readers, for being on my team. Some of you have been reading along for twelve years now, ever since I started a little blog about my life with my toddler boys and newborn daughter. And some of you are newer to the game, but just as dear. This adventure never would have happened without you.

ABOUT THE AUTHOR

Greta Eskridge is a second-generation homeschooling mom who credits her parents with developing lasting bonds with her throughout her childhood years. Her message of deeply connected and intentional parenting began as a blog about her early days of mothering and blossomed into a writing and speaking career that today connects her to the hearts of mothers and fathers across the country. Greta and her husband, Aaron, have been married for twenty-two years and have four children. They strive to fill their lives and the lives of their children with creativity and a passion for the things they value in life: art, books, nature, adventuring, and pursuing deep relationships with family, friends, and God.